VALUES-
BASED
SELLING

The Art of Building
High-Trust Client Relationships
for Financial Advisors, Insurance Agents
and Investment Reps

"When you do business with wealthy, successful clients, building trust is much more important than good selling skills. The strategies taught in this book will help financial advisors at any level build these high-trust relationships on purpose. Bill's ideas coincide completely with our philosophy at Renaissance."

ELTON H. BROOKS
Chairman, Renaissance, Inc.

"Fresh, upbeat, genuine effort to challenge and motivate financial services professionals to move up to a new level of success. I like the book's simplicity and natural, easy-going style. While it's fun and interesting to read, it is also challenging because it raises many significant and important questions."

JOHN CRUIKSHANK
General Agent,
Northwestern Mutual
1997 MDRT President

"This book is must reading for any financial professional who wants to succeed at his or her highest level."

GRANT SYLVESTER
President, Money Concepts
Canada Ltd.

"Finally! A book that teaches the specifics of how and why clients trust you and what to do to earn it, keep it and get an endless stream of referrals because of it."

JOHN BOWEN
CEO, Reinhardt, Werba, Bowen

"The game has changed in sales. Bill Bachrach's relationship orientation is a mission critical to building trust with today's sophisticated customers."

GREG LINK
Vice-President of
Business Development,
Covey Leadership Center

"Excellent follow-up to the audio/video Learning System."

ROSS KASNER
Northwestern Mutual Life

"Since working with Bill Bachrach and his Values-Based Selling process, my business has exploded! Bill's process is the finest financial training program I have ever seen and worked with. This tremendous book is very important to sales professionals because it enables them to understand the sales process and unlock their potential by using the Values-Based Selling concepts."

DAVID KUTCHER
DAK Financial Group
Court of the Table MDRT

"Brilliant! I've known for a long time that our buying decisions are dictated by our value system, but I've never before seen such a simple system of discovering exactly what those values are in others and how to relate them to my services as a professional. I think the Values-Based Selling concept could become one of the most significant contributions to improving the quality of our industry to come around in a long time. You have hit a Grand Slam Home Run!"

JOE CHENOWETH
Director of Advanced Marketing,
Ackley Financial

"Your Values-Based Selling process is one of the most innovative tools I have seen in my 23 years of recruiting. In addition, the sales managers report that the case work is easier because the agents are bringing them better and more complete fact finders. The result of this is that we are down from four–five field appointments to two–three per client presentation. Your process is very important to our success."

JOHN R. HALSEY, LUTCF
General Agent,
John Hancock

"I am presenting this book to our seasoned sales force."

PETER BROERSMA
President,
Financial Concept Group

"Congratulations! Your work is outstanding. Values-Based Selling should provide anyone interested in going to the next level a concise blueprint or a road map on how to successfully accomplish their goals. A must read!"

JOBY GRUBER
Sr. Vice-President, Chief
Marketing Services Officer, FSC

"Bill Bachrach can open new paradigms for you in developing a deep relationship with your clients. The first chapter alone on picking your clients is worth the price of the book."

RICHARD AVERITT
Sr. Vice-President, National Sales
Manager, IM&R

"Values-Based Selling is a proven, transferable method for earning trust and learning how to use it to a client's benefit. This book is excellent by itself or as a terrific companion to Bill Bachrach's Learning System."

MARK ROGERS
Sr. Vice-President, MFS

"In our business we ask people to give us their money and then pay us to take it. Before they do that there has to be trust. This book explains how to build trust quickly and on purpose! I wish I had this available to me 19 years ago when I first started in this business. It's a must read for the serious financial planning professional."

MARK MERSHON, CFP, ChFC, CLU
President,
Triple Check Financial Services

"This is the ultimate client relationship–building handbook for the financial services industry. Buy it. Read it. Implement what you learn immediately."

RICHARD A. HOLLAR, CLU
Sr. Executive Vice-President of
Marketing, The Old Line Life
Insurance

"The results have been profound and measurable. The bottom line is that my production was about $200,000 gross and this year I will have a 75% increase."

HAROLD L. HIGGINS
Vice-President of Investments,
A. G. Edwards

"The industry needs this book, particularly the part about leading by example. The workbook format allows for maximum participation."

LEO WELLS
President, Wells Capital, Inc.

"Your Values-Based Selling process is one of the most creative and effective ways of dealing with prospects and clients that I have ever seen. Your ideas are highly transferable and immediately usable. I have also found that they are cost-effective to implement in the field and just make good sense.

"We have adopted the Values-Based Selling model and are moving our field force toward a focus on the client rather than the product. The results are good for everyone. We no longer approach the client with a single transaction mind set. We have many producers who are having success each day with your methods and ideas."

DAVE FREITAG
Vice-President of Agencies,
Allmerica Financial

"This book is a 'must have' for people who aspire to be the leaders in the financial services industry. You have truly given us a method/process to achieve greatness. Thank you!"

NED DANE
National Sales Desk Manager,
Putnam Mutual Funds

"This book is great! It goes beyond theory to provide how-to information vital for survival in today's marketplace."

TIMOTHY SULLIVAN
MONY

"After attending your Values-Based Selling program, I began using your WIA —— TY process right away. I used it with a business owner who got so excited about the process and us working together he said, 'I am going to line your pockets with gold from all the business I am going to give you and send you.'"

STUART REILLY
Smith Barney Shearson

"I found your process creates quicker relationships, and they are more open. Rather then people saying to me, 'Let me think about what we are talking about. I will get back to you,' I have found they say, 'Yes, we would like to go ahead and start the planning process now. What do we need to do?'"

HERBERT T. HANSON, CFP, ChFC
Financial Planning
Services, Inc./FSC

"My production increased 40% the first full year after hearing your presentation and implementing the WIA —— TY question. I used to be very detail oriented, logical and product oriented. Now I am having much more fun, getting closer to my clients, feeling better about what I do and how it helps people— in addition to increasing my personal earnings."

FRANK A. AUSK, JR.
Allmerica Financial

"It used to take me an hour and a half in a client meeting to really feel satisfied that trust had been built but now that I use your 'values conversation,' it takes only 12 minutes to gain my client's trust. Not only that, but I know exactly what I did to earn their trust so I can easily duplicate the process every time. Your analogy of the sales supercharger is perfect: it saves time while improving results and confidence."

MICHAEL J. HELGESEN, CFP, R.H.U.
Agency Manager, AIG Life
Insurance

"As proof of your Values-Based Selling process' effectiveness, my total weighted production for December was over $1 million, most of it coming after I attended your seminar. It works!"

PETER S. VIROK
American Express
Financial Advisors

"At last! Bill teaches us how to build trust quickly, ethically and on purpose. This is a book you have been waiting to read—it is a must read for those people who are serious about moving to the next level."

RICHARD A. KOOB, CLU, ChFC
Northwestern Mutual Life

"A surprising aspect of your approach is that its results are almost instantaneous. In a short period of time you are able to accomplish a high level of trust and openness."

REGINA BEDOYA
Prudential

"Stimulating! A well-thought-out plan that is providing direction for people searching for growth in improving their professional skills."

J. MANLEY DENTON
VP-OSL Sales, Ohio State Life

"In the 15 years I have been in the financial services industry, I have never seen anything that I feel will impact my future in this business like your Values-Based Selling. It provides a complete turn-key system that anyone can follow. You really hit a HOME RUN with the book and I feel very fortunate to have been one of the people to get it before its actual publication."

GARY BLEVINS, CFP
Blevins Financial Group

"Is selling an uphill battle for you? Bill Bachrach's trust-building principles are your bible to downhill selling."

THOMAS C. HANSCH, CFP, CLU
President, Financial Profiles

"Every new client I have seen since I started using your material has committed to do a plan with me within 15 minutes of being in my office, 100%. The warm, fuzzy feelings I am now able to create make us feel like we've known each other forever. They are so committed to do the process, they get their financial data back to me within two days instead of the weeks it sometimes used to drag on. Thanks!"

BOB PISCURA, CFP
American Express
Financial Advisors

"Your book teaches the lessons I've learned over the past 32 years of building a successful insurance, estate and retirement practice. It focuses on the most important lesson of all: 'Trust is king' in the financial services profession. Then it teaches a proven method for a trustworthy person to build trust. I wish I had had the opportunity to read it 30 years ago."

DON R. SCHAFER, CLU
New York Life

"The first year I began implementing Values-Based Selling I was able to take all of July and August off to be with my family, and my production went up too."

KEN FRIEDMAN
American Express
Financial Advisors

"Bill's book clearly addresses a void in the marketplace today. Truly worth the investment of time for anybody serious about improving their interpersonal skills."

BILL KREBS
Divisional Insurance Sales
Manager, Merrill Lynch
Insurance Group

"I used your referral approach with one of my 'Great Clients' and her response was, 'Sure, I know a lot of people who would value the work you have done for me over the past two years.' I can't wait to meet with my other 19 'Great Clients' and get their referrals!"

PRICE CHIPLEY FRENCH
The Potter Financial Group

"I used the Values Conversation with a client I have had for 10 years and got $23 million more assets."

DONNA BEERS
FNIC

"I have never had such success as I have with your process. I made $70,000 within the last two weeks just for starters!"

PETE RAY
SunAmerica Securities

"Values-Based Selling helped me generate over $60,000 of fees in January alone!"

DAVID BACH
Dean Witter

"As a result of implementing your WIA ——— TY process, clients give me complete fact-finder information, and that means they trust me. I get through all the barriers real quick so I have significantly reduced the time it takes to bond with clients."

DONALD CINOCCO
Prudential

"I have been Top of The Table producer for five years and have never seen anything as powerful as your process. It will help me be even more successful in a much shorter time."

ROBERT N. HAMILTON, CLU, ChFC
Aetna Investment Services, Inc.

"I use your WIA ——— TY process in the initial discussion. It works! It gets agreement and commitment a lot quicker. I differentiate myself because nobody else asks my prospects and clients the questions you teach. Since I have been getting their core values, prospects and clients don't have objections, because their core values lead them to do what they need to do for their reasons."

WILLIAM THARP II
William G. Tharp II
& Associates/FSC

"I use your material with every prospect and client because I know more say yes when I do."

MARGARET LOFARO, CFP
FNIC

"Excellent presentation and process. Stimulates your thinking. Creates a lifelong challenge to be brilliant and balanced."

STEPHEN J. PASCAL
Pascal Insurance Ltd.

"Values-Based Selling motivates and inspires with substance and not empty cheerleading. When the word gets out, I'm sure it will be a bestseller."

GEORGE NOVOTNY

"I used your process with 27 appointments. I closed 25 of the 27 couples and I believe your process had a definite impact!"

MICHAEL E. GOODNER
Prudential

"You have a real winner! Excellent! Sensational! Outstanding! Extraordinary!"

HOMER NOTTINGHAM
Division Vice-President,
American Express
Financial Advisors

"This book is loaded with money-making and relationship-building techniques for financial professionals. Buy it, read it, and implement its ideas and you'll double your income!"

DR. TONY ALESSANDRA
Author, *The Platinum Rule* and
Collaborative Selling

"I admire Bill Bachrach. His Values-Based Selling system is a powerful yet simple tool. With it, you'll gain not only the trust of your clients but also greater confidence in yourself."

JIM CATHCART
Author, *Relationship Selling*

"After hearing the best MDRT speakers for 41 years now, I found your program to be one of the brightest beacons in our industry today. Your process is not only sound in ethical principles, but exceptional in execution. Trust is the key element of success!"

WALTER HANSCH, CLU
Hansch Financial Group

"I have always been successful in developing great business relationships. But since learning and using your trust-building process, my average income per client is up almost 200%!"

TOM OLIVO
T. G. Olivo & Associates

"The clients tend to invest larger amounts and treat me with greater respect than before utilizing your Values-Based Selling approach. My closing ratio has increased dramatically, and I need to talk to far fewer people than before for much better results."

EDWARD J. BUDREIKA
Assoc. Vice-President,
Sintra Capital Group, Inc.

"I have been in the business for 23 years. Your program is the most incredible relationship-building process I have ever seen. My seminar buying unit–to–appointment ratio went from 50% to 70%!"

WILLIAM DeMORROW
WCD Financial, Inc.

"Not only did I gain the trust of my prospect, I walked out with apps and checks for two incentive life policies that put $4200 into my pocket!"

JEFFREY LIPSCOMMB
The Equitable

"I have truly differentiated myself from the rest, and that has increased my business and shortened the amount of time it takes with each prospect. I have used your process on high income people and they are 'blown away' because nobody ever asked them these questions before."

ROBERT A. EBERT, J.D.
Advanced Financial
Concepts/Royal Alliance

"The agents who tried your approach cannot believe the results. It's a totally unique approach that works like a charm and really does add value to the sale and the relationship."

ROBERT E. HOFFMAN, CLU, ChFC
Advanced Sales Consultant,
Canada Life

"Your Values-Based recruiting process reduces the time it takes to recruit a qualified candidate by 50%."

R. ED DULEY
General Agent,
Allmerica Financial

"I have used your Values-Based Selling process with every new client. As a result, I have gotten very detailed fact finders from every one of them."

J. TOWNSEND GILBERT
National Life of Vermont

"Your approach is terrific! I'm getting appointments with people I'd been trying to see for years."

WILLIAM A. HARRIS
Alchemy Investment
Planning/Royal Alliance

"I use your process to help my producers close more business faster. One example is when, after a couple of phone calls with a client and one face-to-face meeting, he gave us his 401(k) in excess of $1 million."

PATRICK MURPHY
Delaware Group

"You teach a way to communicate with clients more effectively and on a deeper level. As a result, I have been able to discover clients' 'real' needs and meet them more quickly."

RICH MORAN
Registry Financial Planner, FNIC

"Right after I saw your program, I used your Values-Based Selling process. I used WIA —— TY with six people, five on the phone and one in person. I got exactly the positive response you talked about in your program. I found a way to totally dominate my area!"

GLENN BEVER
FSC

"After being introduced to your Values-Based Selling process, I went back to a few hard-to-sell cases and got the business! In a short period of time I made over $18,000 in commissions from these two cases that I would not have gotten without using your process."

RONALD QUICK
John Hancock

"Since using your process, I've been able to dramatically shorten my sales cycle and significantly enhance client relationships. I'm getting more and bigger sales because your approach puts the emphasis on the client/advisor relationship rather than selling products."

DAVID SCHNEIDER
Robert Thomas Securities

"I did not read Values-Based Selling; *I devoured it! Without a doubt, this book will serve as the definitive hands-on, specific methodology for financial professionals from now on."*

BRUNO A. GIORDANO
President, Dorset Financial
Services Corp.

"I use your Values-Based Selling process with existing clients and prospects. It has definitely led to a lot more sales. I attribute at least a 50% increase in my business because of your system. Thanks!"

DREW MALKIN
New Jersey Life & Casualty

VALUES-BASED SELLING

The Art of Building
High-Trust Client Relationships
for Financial Advisors, Insurance Agents
and Investment Reps

Bill Bachrach

AIM HIGH PUBLISHING
San Diego, California

Aim High Publishing
8380 Miramar Mall, Suite 200
San Diego, CA 92121

First edition 1996
Ninth printing 2002

Designed by Robert Mott & Associates • Keswick, Virginia
Illustrated by Tom Klare • San Diego, California
Edited by Just Write • Keswick, Virginia
Printed in the United States of America

ISBN 1-887006-00-1

Trademarked Words

The following terms in this book are trademarked by Bachrach &
Associates, Inc: The Financial Road Map, Four Quadrants, High-Trust
Leadership, The Success Road Map, Trusted Advisor, Trusted Advisor
Coach, Values-Based Financial Plan, Values-Based Financial Planning,
Values-Based Financial Professional, Values-Based Selling, Values
Conversation, Values Staircase and Being Done.

For Anne

Acknowledgments

I want to thank God for creating curiosity, being sure I had an abundance of it and bringing the many people into my life who made this book possible.

I want to thank the inventors of the printing press, audio- and videotape and the computer because they created the vehicles that can give anyone an advantage who chooses to capitalize on the knowledge available.

Thank you, Anne, for encouraging me to write this book.

I thank my parents for their love, their prayers and for raising me with the freedom to chart my own course instead of trying to chart one for me. (Even when I know they sometimes thought I should have finished college and gotten a "real" job.)

I thank my mentors, formal and informal, who taught me many, many things. Foremost, they taught me to invest in my most important asset—myself. Thank you for helping me discover my true purpose. Thank you for seeing things in me before I saw them in myself. And I thank you for your patience in the face of my never-ending questions.

Thank you, Elizabeth, Karen and Deena, for taking charge of this project and bringing your knowledge and writing skills to the table so this book could become a reality. I hope I wasn't the most difficult client you've ever had, as I'm sure I wasn't the easiest.

Thank you, Tom Klare, for the illustrations.

Thank you, Robert Mott, for creative design and cover ideas.

Thank you, Paula, for your creative ideas and managing the details.

Thank you, Nancy, for your prayers and managing the money.

I thank all the speakers, consultants and authors in the world who have gone before me. Some of you paved the way for what is possible for me to do today and provide great examples of what to aspire to.

Last, and absolutely not least, I thank my clients for proving many, many times over how high and how far Values-Based Selling can take financial professionals who implement its principles. I also thank you for teaching me at least as much as I have taught you.

Contents

PART I   VALUES BASICS ARE YOUR KEYS TO NEVER HAVING TO "SELL"—OR SETTLE—AGAIN.

PART II   ONCE YOU'VE LAID A FOUNDATION OF TRUST, BUILDING YOUR CLIENTS' FINANCIAL FUTURE IS A SNAP.

PART III   GETTING IT WAS ONE THING. KEEPING IT IS EVERYTHING.

APPENDIXES—MORE PATHS TO MASTERY

Preface

Although financial services can be a difficult, unpredictable business, one of the most exciting things about it is that you have total control over your life. You can make a lot of money without taking the entire year to earn it. Your income, your free time, your family's quality of life, the fulfillment of your values and the achievement of your dreams are totally up to you.

If you are proud of your career so far, you deserve the credit. If your career to this point has not been as successful as you would like, then you have only yourself to blame—don't blame your company, compliance requirements, your manager, the poor financial habits of the country's citizens, the state of the industry, the economy, politics, unrest in the Middle East or the biased media. You are responsible for your own career choices and their consequences—good and bad.

This is great news! It means you have the power now to move beyond your current level of success and make your career and your life exactly what you want them to be. No excuses. Failing with an excuse (even a really, really good one) is never as good as succeeding. If you have decided to succeed at your highest potential, rather than make excuses, the information in this book will help you get there.

Have you ever been frustrated because you seem to care more about your clients' financial future than they seem to care themselves?

Have you ever progressed well into a relationship before discovering undisclosed assets and then wondered why your clients didn't give you all the information in the first interview?

Have you ever worked very hard to convince someone to become a client and later wished you hadn't?

Have you ever wondered why you have to do so much prospecting and marketing for new business when you have a base of great clients who could be giving you enough referrals to keep your calendar full?

When you choose to master Values-Based Selling, you eliminate all these frustrations and enter a whole new realm of business. As a result of reading this book, I hope you come to realize that your job is *not* to choose the right stocks, mutual funds, asset-management service, annuities or best insurance contracts, but rather to guide your clients to achieve their long-term goals and fulfill their core values. It's not about performance or having the lowest costs. Think *process* not products, *relationships* not transactions.

I hope this book motivates you to embark on a journey toward being brilliant at creating high-trust client relationships. Such relationships have some distinctive characteristics:

- **You quickly earn the trust of great clients.**
- **You easily obtain full disclosure.** At the first meeting, prospects tell you where all their money is and candidly discuss their goals.
- **You always get commitment before you do the work.** You never work on false hopes about what will happen when you prepare and present your ideas. People keep their commitments and implement your recommendations.

- **You comfortably ask for and receive good referrals.** When clients trust you and are impressed with your work, they are happy to introduce you to their friends, relatives and colleagues. Soon, you will have a 100% referral-based business.

- **You are extremely effective on the phone.** People make and keep their appointments, and they bring all their financial documents to the first meeting.

- **You take control of your career.** You never fear losing clients because of events outside your control. Your client relationships are based on something bigger than stock market fluctuations, economic changes, company ratings, interest rate volatility, the opinions of friends and relatives or negative press reports. Your clients are more influenced by their trust in you than by all outside factors combined.

- **You efficiently weed out the time wasters.** There will still be people who won't do business with you, but you'll find that out in the first five minutes and get rid of them right away. This results in amazing time savings, stress reduction and increased confidence.

- **You build a better life for yourself and your family.** You earn more money in less time, and it feels good to help people move down the path of financial success and security. You are happier and healthier because you are able to do good work for people who appreciate your efforts, and you have more time and money to achieve your own goals and fulfill your own core values.

I invite you to incorporate all these characteristics into your client relationships on purpose and consistently. This is what Values-Based Selling has done for many professionals. This is what it can do for you.

Introduction— The Next Level

The premise of this book is that everyone has a next level of success—whether they're just starting out, already established or eminently successful. This book is written for serious financial professionals who are always looking to achieve their own unique next level. Obviously, yours may not be the same as mine or anyone else's. Achieving *your* next level could be about any of the following:

- Earning more income
- Having more time off
- Becoming financially independent
- Being debt-free
- Enjoying peak physical health
- Having total security or freedom
- Being a better parent, husband or wife
- Having a sense of accomplishment and pride
- Attaining spiritual fulfillment
- Making a contribution to humanity
- Being respected by your peers and clients
- Having a life of significance not just success

If you think about it, you realize that the success of your business impacts everything on this list, either directly or indirectly. The more successful your business becomes, the more time and the less stress you have in the other important aspects of your life. **The purpose of this book is to help you attain your next level of success, no matter how you define it.**

Trust Is the Key.

Trust is the single most important prerequisite for creating client relationships that produce big results with less time and effort. However, most training in the financial services industry emphasizes products and sales. There's no *trust training*. Yet you have probably noticed that **when you are trusted, you don't need anything you learned about sales.** Sales training addresses the symptoms, not the problem. When people don't respond to your advice, they are really telling you they don't trust you enough to take action on your ideas. When they choose not to open up, tell you the truth about their current financial situation and be candid about their needs, goals and problems, it's because they do not trust you enough to do so. When they rebuff your approach, they are telling you they do not believe you have their best interests at heart. These clients are not telling you that you need to make better features and benefits presentations, handle their objections more cleverly or be a smoother "closer." *There's simply no trust.*

While sales training continues to focus on symptoms, this book addresses the underlying problem and provides solutions. Much like preventive medicine keeps you out of the hospital in the first place, Values-Based Selling will keep you out of the common tug-of-war of convincing, persuading and selling reluctant people on ideas that benefit them more than they benefit you.

Of course, it's important to be good at what you d
and to know your products, but you have probably als
noticed that few, if any, people have failed in this busir
because they lacked product knowledge. Many fail,
however, because they are not effective at rapidly building
the high-trust client relationships that lead to consistent
business, repeat business and referrals.

By applying what you learn in *Values-Based Selling*, you
will develop the ability to build trust quickly with people
who will make good clients. You will also be prepared to
determine rapidly if a prospect will not be a good client
and, therefore, disengage immediately if necessary.

Right now you are probably wasting time trying to
do business with people who will never be good clients.
Channel that time into the right business relationships
and you will experience a quantum leap in productivity
and satisfaction, no matter how successful you are already.

Your values-based clientele will consist of your ideal
clients: people who tell you where all their money is in the
first meeting, make commitments to become your clients
for life, consistently keep their commitments, introduce
you to everyone they know who meets *your* standards and
do what you advise them to do. **The key to attaining your
ideal clientele is the art of deliberately and sincerely
building trust.** That is the single most important
ingredient in any business relationship. If you are not
building high-trust client relationships on purpose, you
are selling by accident. As long as you choose to sell by
accident, you cannot achieve your highest level of success.

Most top producers I have encountered don't really
know what causes a prospect to trust or distrust them,
so although they do very well, many of the best in our
business still sell by accident. The development of trust is
often attributed to chemistry, intuition, gut feeling, long-
term effort, being honest, product performance or some
other unexplained, accidental or mysterious process such

as, "I just *exude* trustworthiness." This guesswork makes it difficult to approach trust building methodically, and seldom is any effort made to teach financial professionals *how* to build trust deliberately.

The most professional selling skills in the hands of highly ethical financial professionals can undermine client trust instead of earning it. For example, the old-school, manipulative tactics of selling to fear or greed create the wrong emotions to build trust. Even the commonly taught rapport techniques (like beginning a client interview with small talk, common ground, superficial chitchat or credentials and company strength) often work against the most well-meaning financial professional. Using these sales techniques, even with good intentions, is like tossing an anvil to save someone who is drowning.

"Here, I'll save you!"

Financial professionals who are not building trust on purpose with every client will continue to be frustrated by prospects who need what they are selling but who will not buy. It's not that financial professionals are bad at the game of selling— they're simply playing the wrong game.

A New Era

In the transaction era, financial services was a sales game, and traditional sales techniques worked pretty well. Now, in the era of planning, gathering assets and charging fees, financial services is about building trust and long-term client relationships.

Our industry needs the proven approach of Values-Based Selling now more than ever, not only because times have changed, but because the public trusts us less than ever. We must be able to build trust quickly, ethically and on purpose. Values-Based Selling is not primarily about selling at all; it's about becoming a Values-Based Financial Professional who builds such incredible relationships that people want you to help them with all their financial choices in life. Your clients will then buy what you recommend without ever feeling "sold."

PART I

Values Basics
Are Your Keys to
Never Having
to "Sell"
—or Settle—
Again.

1. Choose Your Clients: Be a Values-Based Financial Professional.

Most financial professionals can only dream of the day when they'll be choosing their clients instead of persuading prospects to buy. But such limited thinking is completely backward. If you want the success of your dreams, then you have to *start by choosing your clients*. Doesn't it make sense to identify prospects who will make you the most successful and to invest in relationships with them instead of spending your time and energy trying to convince everyone to work with you—including people who either can't, won't or shouldn't be your clients?

Maybe it seems unreasonable to expect clients to meet *your* standards, but I've never heard of a company or a financial professional who failed because of setting standards too high.

Becoming a Values-Based Financial Professional, or VBFP, means raising your standards. It means expecting of yourself high levels of production and performance, including creating for your clients a financial future that meets their core values. It also means expecting your clients to be more committed to their financial future than you are and expecting them to show that commitment by congruent behavior.

Values-Based Selling is built on a brief exchange with prospects about the importance of money in their lives. This "values conversation" is the subject of Chapter 2. It starts with the simple question, "What's important about money *to you?*" The conversation sparked by this one question is the single most powerful way to establish a high-trust relationship, and it is the quickest way to determine whether (or not) you want someone to become a client.

In other words, the values conversation provides a reliable method for discovering within the first five minutes of your first interview whether a prospect is worth pursuing. Imagine what life would be like if you worked only with clients who told you the truth, kept commitments, gave referrals, and did everything you advised them to do! It's possible if you weed out the time wasters early.

To do this, you have three simple objectives for the first meeting:

1. Determine whether prospects are in or out. (They're out if they can't or won't trust you, or if they prove uncooperative.)

2. If they're in, discover where all their money is and prioritize their financial goals.

3. Have them make a commitment to do business with you (or not).

In pursuing these objectives, the discriminating financial professional will recognize five types of clients: the Great Client, the Sometimes Worth Helping Client, the Fun but Hopeless Client, the Uses You for Information Client, and the Doesn't Trust Anybody Client. The first two are your Holy Grail. The last three are trouble: They will be difficult clients if they slip through your filter.

1. The Great Client

Great clients are coachable and financially responsible. They want to manage their money intelligently. **These people are receptive to dealing with a financial professional because their time is precious and they like having business** *relationships.* They are busy working on their own career success, running a business or, as happy retirees, doing what they enjoy. Because Great Clients are good at their own profession, they respect others who also excel. To spot a potential Great Client, look for some particular qualities in the prospects you screen:

- They like participating in the values conversation, discussing their goals and clarifying their current financial situation.
- They see the whole process of creating a financial strategy as exciting and important.

- They are grateful to find someone who is trustworthy, competent and knowledgeable to help them with their financial choices.
- They bring their documents to the first meeting or make sure the financial professional receives them quickly.

Great Clients are not pushovers or "lay downs." They are just straightforward and sincere, and they don't play games. They should be the lifeblood of your business, people you genuinely care about and require a valuable service and whose trust you hold as a privilege and foundation of your relationship.

2. The Sometimes Worth Helping Client

Some people have good intentions but struggle to stay on track. A relationship with them may be profitable, but you have to make a judgment call. The Sometimes Worth Helping are not yet Great Clients, but they do have potential. They tend to be people who

- sound a lot like Great Clients but are weak in follow-through,
- need more hand holding,
- hesitate to make commitments.

With this type of client, you must be very firm. You cannot tolerate any deviation from commitments. **Those who are Sometimes Worth Helping need someone in their lives who will encourage them to do what they**

know will be wise for the long term. If you have ever struggled with a diet, an exercise program or your own savings plan, you understand how these people feel.

Beware of wasting too much time with these people. You will find that they need your strength and discipline more than anything else you can give them.

3. The Fun but Hopeless Client

You already know some of these charmers. They are great to socialize with because they love spending their money. Unfortunately, these genuinely nice people make lousy clients, no matter how much money they earn. **If only they could invest as well as they rationalize ("You only live once!" "You can't take it with you!" "Money can't buy happiness!"), they would be very, very rich.**

Given a little practice, you will recognize the warning signs that certain of your prospects are Fun but Hopeless. These people share the following characteristics:

- They appear sincere and motivated during the meetings but never follow through.

- They are reluctant to share the details of their financial condition.

- They are smart enough to know they are digging their own financial grave, but lack the discipline to change their "fatal" habits.

- They may be cavalier about their financial future because of an expected inheritance or benefactor.

- They sometimes are burdened with so much debt that they are embarrassed to tell you the truth about it.

- They rarely get their financial documents to you, no matter how many times you ask and they promise.

- They think having a good excuse for not getting their financial life together is as good as having a sound financial strategy.

- They have a lifestyle that is much bigger than their financial reality.

- They tend to be unrealistically optimistic.

Harry Kasanow, a VBFP in Hawaii, told *USA Today* this story about two Fun but Hopeless clients: Together, the couple makes $300,000 per year, but they have no savings except the husband's pension at work. Harry put them on a budget, and at the end of the first year they had managed to save $14,000. Harry congratulated them, saying, "I'm proud of you. You saved $14,000 this year." The clients said, "Fantastic! We saved $14,000! Let's celebrate! Let's spend that $14,000 and take the whole family to Europe!"

A few Fun but Hopeless Clients might become Great Clients at some point, perhaps when they're 55 years old and realize they have only ten years to save for retirement. A Fun but Hopeless can wake up—the question is whether you're willing to hang around for that remote possibility.

4. The Uses You for Information Client

These people have the discipline to manage their own money, and they enjoy doing research. **They use financial professionals for information, and then they buy their investments or insurance from the cheapest source.** They believe this approach is perfectly legitimate. They may have such low opinions of financial professionals that they have no qualms at all about taking advantage of them.

These manipulators do not make good clients unless they are awfully rich and sometimes throw a bone to the financial professional they use for information. Even then, it's probably not worth it. Bones are for dogs, and your self-worth is a more valuable asset than any one client. You can recognize people who are using you for information because they exhibit some typical characteristics:

- They either refuse to answer any questions in the interview by saying something like, "Just tell me what you have!" Or they are too eager to give you details so they can quickly obtain a solution from you: "Here's my situation. What would you do?"

- They engage in nonproductive philosophical conversations about commissions, compensation, or some irrelevant article in a recent newspaper.

- They like to discuss no-load funds, market timing and investment philosophy.

9

- They are often clever enough to make you question whether your approach is reasonable.
- They tend to play devil's advocate, taking either side in any issue.
- They seem to derive their self-worth from getting something for nothing.
- They are more interested in showing you how smart they are than in really seeking your help.

The best you can do for yourself is to identify these users quickly and run.

5. The Doesn't Trust Anybody Client

These distrusting people always expect to be betrayed. In their minds, danger lurks around the next corner. I won't delve into the psychological problems these people must have, but suffice it to say that financial professionals aren't qualified to provide the kind of counseling they need. Don't try. Instead, protect yourself by watching out for these people:

- They say they don't trust anybody and treat you suspiciously from the start. (You are "guilty until proven innocent.")
- They have many stories about how their business relationships always sour.
- They are suspicious when you ask the questions you need to ask in order to help them.

- They just "know" there is an angle there somewhere, and they only need a little time to find it.

The best you can do for yourself is to recognize these nontrusters quickly, feel a little sorry for them and leave them to their paranoia.

Know the Difference!

Your profit and satisfaction come from the Great Clients (whom you always want) and the Sometimes Worth Helping Clients (whom you sometimes want but who require a judgment call). Your problems and frustration come from the client who is Fun but Hopeless, Uses You for Information, or Doesn't Trust Anybody.

Disengaging from Difficult People

You probably agree in principle that it is best to avoid the prospect who is Fun but Hopeless, Uses You for Information, or Doesn't Trust Anybody. But you may not have had training in how to show the prospect politely to the door. Not only is this a skill you can and should learn, but it can also be an enjoyable, empowering experience.

I've met many successful financial professionals who are uncomfortable disengaging, and some of them have never shown a prospect to the door. I'm always amazed by that, but it seems they don't do so because they're hoping the person will become easier to deal with. They incorrectly take responsibility: They think that maybe the prospect isn't really difficult and instead blame themselves for not saying or doing the right thing. So how do you know where the problem lies when a prospect is being difficult? Is it you or the prospect?

One of the key benefits of becoming a VBFP and mastering the values conversation is how well these techniques flush out people you don't want to do business with and build relationships with the people you do want to do business with. The only challenge is that you have to be very good; otherwise, you can't tell if the reason things aren't working is your lack of skill or the prospect is someone you want to disengage from. When you are highly skilled and things aren't working, you know it must be them.

Be careful not to prematurely blame your new skills when a prospect or client doesn't respond as well as you would like. Blaming Values-Based Selling when things don't work well would be like Shaquille O'Neal blaming the basketball hoop when he missed a free throw. The hoop didn't move; he just missed.

You will discover that the question that initiates all Values-Based Selling—"What's important about money *to you?*"—doesn't "move," either; it's the right one at the right time. That's part of the power of being a VBFP: **You can easily identify the difficult people and feel good about disengaging from them.** Here's what to say when you want to disengage.

> **VBFP.** [*Extending a hand.*] I don't think this is going to work. I've found that I need the clients I accept to be in a position to have a high

level of commitment to their future. It is clear you are not ready at this point in time, and that's OK. You have my number. If things change, feel free to give me a call.

[*Preparing to graciously escort the prospect out of the office.*]

If you have ever disengaged from prospective clients, you know that the person is usually shocked. The majority of the time, you may hear a response like this:

Prospect. What do you mean?

VBFP.   You don't seem to want to answer my questions or cooperate in the process. It's your choice, but if you don't answer my questions then I can't help you, so there's no point in moving forward.

Prospect. I'm sorry. I'll answer your questions. I didn't mean to be difficult.

You can then decide whether or not to give the prospect a second chance.

This is not a manipulative ploy to get people to want to work with you. Nor is it a new version of the "take-away" close. The point is not to play games to get a prospect to cooperate. **The point is that the VBFP assumes a position of someone with high standards who doesn't waste time with cynical, uncooperative people.** You are making a point about your principles and rules for doing business. People

13

are attracted to others who have high standards and principles.

It's OK to end an unproductive relationship. Most of the successful financial professionals I know say they wish they had learned this lesson early in their careers. Appropriately disengaging increases your success whether you are a brand-new financial professional or have been in the business for 25 years. You are far better off spending your time looking for a cooperative client than trying to convert a difficult one.

> *"I don't know the secret to success. But the key to failure is trying to please everybody."*
>
> BILL COSBY

It may seem odd to you that the first chapter of a book about developing client relationships would teach you how to "blow off" business relationships before they begin, even if you prospected very hard to get the appointment. Yet saying no to the wrong people is just as important as pursuing business relationships with the right ones.

Feeling Good About Letting Go

If you have never turned away a prospect, you are missing one of the finest feelings this business has to offer. If you have been trained to "never turn down a sale," you may have some problems disengaging from the difficult person. To get you over that hurdle, I suggest three reasons that justify politely guiding the difficult person out of your office.

1. More Money

By deliberately choosing to deal only with those clients who are interested in a high-trust lifetime relationship, you are setting and adhering to high standards for yourself and your profession. When prospects just want to buy an insurance policy or invest some money in a mutual fund, let someone else help them. **You don't want customers who buy only one service or product; you want clients who are serious about managing their financial future and who trust you to help them do it.** The best clients want a strategy and a relationship. When they say yes they are agreeing to more than a single transaction or product. Why waste a perfectly good yes on just one sale? By working only with Great Clients you'll make more money because you'll gather all their assets; *you'll be their single financial resource.* That means you will get paid for many different transactions with this client, not just for one sale for one need.

15

2. Higher Self-Esteem

There is power in walking away from difficult people. By saying "This won't work out," you increase your feelings of self-worth. You affirm, "Hey, I don't need this kind of client." After the feelings of discomfort pass, you'll find elation on the other side. You don't need to tolerate difficult people to be successful. In fact, if you are dealing with a lot of difficult people, you are hindering your own success.

MARKET LEADERS BUILD RELATIONSHIPS

"Customer-intimate companies take the long view. . . . So they avoid or shed clients that don't have deep relationship potential. Thus, the customer-intimate company must be able to distinguish the mirage from the real, and it must be willing to walk away from business that might generate only short-term revenues."

MICHAEL TREACY
AND FRED WIERSEMA
Authors of *The Discipline of the Market Leaders*

3. More Referrals

By avoiding difficult, high-maintenance clients, you give yourself time to do more work for cooperative, trusting, low-maintenance clients. And these clients, who are committed to their financial success, are the ones who deserve and appreciate your time and efforts. The better value and service you provide to these people, the more referrals you get. They will do your prospecting and marketing for you.

You may be asking yourself an important question at this point: "Won't I feel bad if I give up on a prospect, even a difficult one?" You can find the answer to this question in the following story.

Incredibly excited, a financial planner who had attended one of my seminars called my office. I was poised to hear a great testimonial about a huge account or insurance case he had landed using Values-Based Selling. Instead he told me he had just used the values conversation, immediately recognized a difficult person and successfully disengaged. He had set the stage for the values conversation and asked the first question beautifully, and the prospect had given him a hard time. He handled the resistance tactfully and with respect and asked the question again, but the client's responsiveness got worse, not better.

Normally he would have felt frustrated that he wasn't "good enough" to say the magic words that could turn this prospect around. However, because of his newfound confidence in the values-based approach, he said, "Look, I'm a qualified financial planner, and if the questions I am asking weren't important, I wouldn't ask them. I appreciate your coming to see me, but it's obvious this isn't going to work out."

He politely escorted the problem prospect to the door. He was elated!

He said, "That was the first time in four years that I really felt in control of my business." Imagine his confidence for the rest of his career, now that he knows how to take charge.

Picture it: You regularly meet with prescreened prospects who fit your ideal client profile—and you simply select the ones you want to work with. Your existing client base is so loyal that they have recommended every one of these "warm" prospects. You are a model of the principles you advise your clients to follow, and other people in your profession respect your advice and counsel. Your time off seems to grow in direct proportion to your escalating income.

Values-Based Selling can help you take control of your career. You have the right and the power to refuse to spend time with difficult people. You will make more money and enjoy a better quality of life by deliberately choosing your clients. It's your career and it's your life; take charge of both of them.

In the next two chapters, you will learn the values conversation. This conversation is an effective method for building high-trust relationships with the right clients and quickly weeding out the wrong ones.

Summary

- You can and should choose your clients.
- Find and pursue the Great Clients and the Sometimes Worth Helping.
- Stay away from the Fun but Hopeless, Uses You for Information and Doesn't Trust Anybody Clients.
- The benefits of avoiding difficult clients include more money, higher self-esteem and more good referrals.

Go through all your client files (or select a portion of them, such as AÑE). As you scan their records and recall your encounters with them, quickly classify each client as a Great Client, a Sometimes Worth Helping Client, a Fun but Hopeless Client, a Uses You for Information Client, or a Doesn't Trust Anybody Client.

Now write down the names of all those clients who fit the last three categories (Fun but Hopeless, Uses You for Information, and Doesn't Trust Anybody). These are probably frustrating or difficult clients who make your life miserable. Are you ready to let them go?

If your answer is either a resounding "Yes!" or a "Yes, but . . ." take the following steps. (What do you have to lose?)

1. From the list of names, choose your most difficult client (the one who most makes your life miserable and gives the least in return for your efforts).

2. Review the warning signs on pages 7–11 for the appropriate category for this client (Fun but Hopeless, Uses You for Information, or Doesn't Trust Anybody.)

3. Call the client and use the warning signs as criteria to verify that he or she really does belong in one of those "difficult people" categories.

4. If the client truly is Fun but Hopeless, Uses You for Information, or Doesn't Trust Anybody, explain that you are restructuring your business plan and you are no longer the best financial professional for him or her right now.

Here's an example: "I have made the decision to focus my services on multiple-service financial plans, and I will be working exclusively with those individuals who are 100% committed. If your position changes in the future, please feel free to call me. Otherwise, I will be happy to forward a copy of your current financial statements to your new financial professional."

NOTES

_____

_____

_____

_____

_____

_____

_____

_____

_____

_____

_____

_____

_____

_____

_____

_____

_____

_____

_____

_____

_____

_____

_____

2. Make the Most of the First Five Minutes.

At the heart of Values-Based Selling is the values conversation. This vital exchange allows you to determine prospects' values, tap into their positive emotions and rapidly gain trust—all in the first five minutes of your first meeting. The values conversation will accomplish these vital objectives:

- It will position you as a valuable financial resource, not just another product salesperson.
- It will quickly flush out time wasters.
- It will build trust and establish an emotional bond.
- It will reveal prospects' core values, which motivate them to action more effectively than anything else.
- It will facilitate accurate goal prioritization.
- It will cause prospects to provide total financial disclosure.
- It will result in a commitment to proceed immediately.
- It will improve your relationship with current clients as well as help you understand new prospects.

You will find the values conversation to be a sincere, caring way to open the interview. It is an engaging, meaningful communication. **You can always win when you use the values conversation, but if you don't really care about your prospects, it will not work.** When you do care, either you quickly establish a high-trust relationship with a client who will take action on your ideas, or you quickly dismiss someone who would have wasted your time or become a difficult, unprofitable client.

Salesperson or Trusted Advisor?

It's much easier to create an impression than to change one. When you meet prospects for the first time, they begin to form opinions about you, and you soon become positioned in their minds either as a salesperson or as a trusted advisor. If you follow the old school sales doctrine—"sell them something first, then make them a client"—and lead with a product to meet a single need (such as college funding, long-term care, asset management, retirement or estate planning), you virtually guarantee you'll be pigeonholed as just another salesperson.

Your prospects and clients quickly put you in the "salesperson" or "trusted advisor" position in their minds.

It's difficult to switch from the role of salesperson to the role of a trusted advisor once your sales behavior has caused someone to categorize you as a salesperson. If you want to occupy the trusted advisor "space" in clients' minds, the smartest thing to do is behave like a trusted advisor from the beginning. Taking this position means initiating the values conversation from the start, focusing on strategy instead of products and not falling back on old-school sales techniques.

- **Advisors ask lots of questions and listen.**
- **Advisors engage in meaningful conversations, not superficial chitchat.**
- **Advisors don't have to explain their credentials, because their competence is obvious.**

Gain Trust Quickly by Talking About What's Important.

The two most critical elements in creating profitable client relationships are *emotional involvement* and *trust*. Without emotion, people will not act quickly on your recommendations. Without trust, people will not believe that you are acting in their best interests. To accomplish the goals of the values conversation in the first five minutes of your first interview, you must initiate a *meaningful* conversation with your prospects. When you conduct a meaningful conversation about their values, prospects become emotionally involved. You understand them on a level very few people do, and you can dramatically **shorten the time it takes to gain their trust**.

In contrast to what sales training typically teaches about probing for hot buttons (needs and wants), the values conversation creates a predictable emotional response and deliberately builds trust. Needs, wants and goals refer to the tangible. Values, on the other hand, are intangible. They are pure, undiluted *feelings*. Consider the emotional power of values like freedom, independence, security, pride, providing for family, accomplishment, achievement, balance, making a difference, satisfaction, fulfillment, spiritual attainment, inner peace and self-worth.

Happiness   Control
Significance
Comfort
Power   Freedom
Actualization
Connection
Helping   Self-direction

There are many possible answers to the question, "What's important about money to you?"

26

These are only a few examples of the values your prospects may consider important; you'll find there are many others. **Your job is to uncover these values-based emotions so people can see the relationship between making smart financial decisions and fulfilling their life values.** Needs and wants have the emotional power of a flashlight; values illuminate like halogen stadium lights.

Determining needs, goals or wants requires simple questions: What do you need? What are your goals? What do you want? Discovering values, however, requires a special process, the process of the values conversation.

As you read the upcoming values conversation, notice how the answers are written from the bottom to the top on the values "staircase." The foundational question is, **"What's important about money *to you*?"** We begin with a conversation about money because, of course, the role of the financial professional—whether you sell securities, professional money management, insurance or financial planning—is to help people make smart choices about their money.

My clients like to call "What's important about money *to you*?" the "WIA ——— TY" (wee-at-tee) question. In the values conversation below, notice how the VBFP writes the prospect's answers, as they are given, on the WIA ——— TY stairs starting from the bottom and working to the top:

27

VBFP.   I'm glad we were able to get together today, Terry. You've invested time to meet with me, which tells me that you must be serious about making smart choices about your money. Is that true?

Terry.   Yes, I am.

VBFP.   Help me understand. **What's important about money *to you*?**

Terry.   Well, money gives me *security*.

VBFP.   [*Writing "security" on first step.*] I see.

The values conversation always starts with the question: "What's important about money to you?"

Security

"What's important about money to you?"

What's important about *money* to you?

VBFP. What's important about *security* to you?

Terry. Having security allows me to do what I want to do, when I want to do it. I feel a sense of *freedom*.

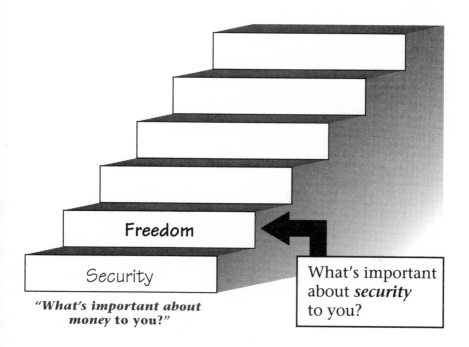

Freedom

Security

"What's important about money to you?"

What's important about *security* to you?

VBFP. Hmmm, that's interesting. Freedom means different things to different people. [*Pausing.*] What's important about *freedom* to you?

Terry. Then I would have more time to *be with my family* and enjoy more *balance* in life.

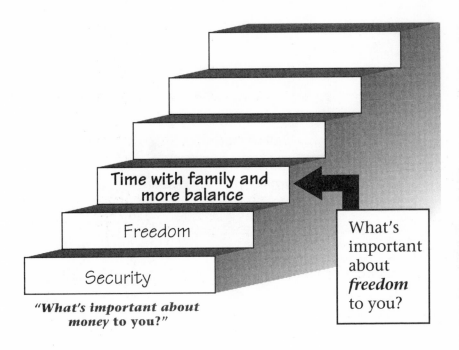

VBFP. OK, Terry, let's assume for a moment you're in the position of having all the time you want to be with your family and enjoy a more balanced life. [*Pausing.*] What's important about being in that position to you?

Terry. I would feel a great *sense of accomplishment.*

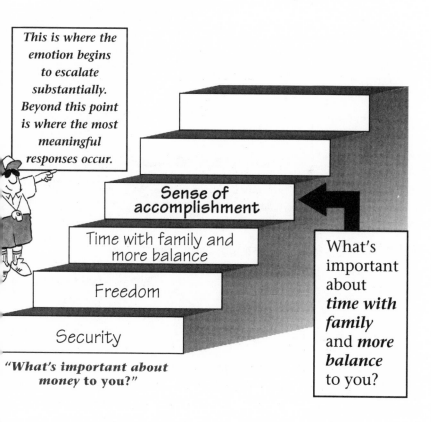

This is where the emotion begins to escalate substantially. Beyond this point is where the most meaningful responses occur.

Sense of accomplishment

Time with family and more balance

Freedom

Security

"What's important about money to you?"

What's important about *time with family* and *more balance* to you?

VBFP.   Accomplishment . . . interesting . . .
give me a little more perspective
on that. [*Pausing.*] What's important about *sense of accomplishment*
to you?

Terry.   Wow, that's tough to answer.
[*Pausing.*]

[VBFP.]   [*Staying silent.*]

Terry.   I guess I get a great sense of
accomplishment from *helping
others* and *making a difference*
in their lives.

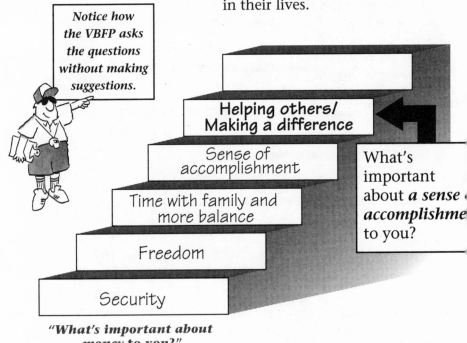

Notice how
the VBFP asks
the questions
without making
suggestions.

Helping others/
Making a difference

Sense of
accomplishment

What's
important
about *a sense*
accomplishme
to you?

Time with family and
more balance

Freedom

Security

"What's important about
money to you?"

VBFP. That's great, Terry. I have only one more question for you right now. [*Pausing.*] What's important about *helping others* and *making a difference* to you, personally?

Terry. Well, that's really what life is all about to me. It makes me feel *satisfied*, like my *life really has purpose*.

VBFP. Is there anything more important to you than the *satisfied* feeling that your life really has *purpose*?

Terry. I don't think so. No.

VBFP. [*Using a slow and deliberate pace to convey that the VBFP has been listening intently and understands the importance and meaning of what Terry has said.*] Terry, suppose we can create a strategy that will

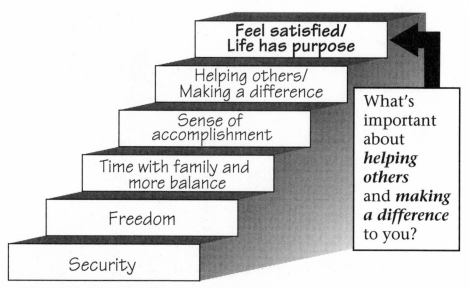

Feel satisfied/
Life has purpose

Helping others/
Making a difference

Sense of
accomplishment

Time with family and
more balance

Freedom

Security

What's important about helping others and making a difference to you?

"What's important about money to you?"

33

help you make smart financial choices. I'm talking about the choices you could make to have the *security* and the *freedom* to *spend more time with your family*, to enjoy the *balance* that allows you to feel a great *sense of accomplishment*, and to *make a difference* for other people so you ultimately have the *sense of satisfaction* that your *life has purpose*. If that were the case, would you and I have a basis for working together?

It's crucial that the VBFP express empathy and compassion, not sounding like a car salesman saying, "If I could show you a way . . ."

Terry. Absolutely.

VBFP. Now that we understand what's important to you, the next step is to get completely clear about your current financial situation and to prioritize your financial goals. Which one would you like to do first?

Check out the nice, smooth transition into fact finding and the financial profile.

Terry. Let's start with my goals. The two things I am very concerned about right now are having enough money to help my kids with college and being able to retire by the time I'm about 60.

The VBFP is now into the financial profile or fact finder.

ANOTHER VALUES-BASED SELLING SUCCESS STORY

"I purchased your tapes on Values-Based Selling at our Masters Conference, and I have been through them several times. I use everything you teach in your system in my interviews.

"One story in particular you will be interested in. Larry, the son of a lady who recently won the lottery, called our office because he is a policy holder with an agent I do joint work with. He wanted to get a 'second opinion' on what his mother should do with her new $1.5 million.

"After going through the WIA ——— TY process with the mother, I went with her to the bank as her financial rep. Following her appointment, we went out for a cup of coffee to discuss all her options. As we were talking about her values, she got tears in her eyes and said, 'I want to work with you.' That commitment gave me $45,000 in commissions and a client for life.

"I guess the money I spent on your Learning System was worth it!

"Before using your process, I always felt like clients trusted me because they knew I cared. Now, I know how to create that emotion on purpose every time, and it's not hit-or-miss anymore. It works every time, no matter what."

DENNIS J. ROGERS, CPA
Allmerica Financial

Use Bridging Comments to Make It Conversational.

To facilitate the values conversation and help smooth the flow, bridging comments are necessary. For example, "Give me some perspective on that" is a bridging comment.

We all know interviews are question-driven conversations. So my rule is this: **If it doesn't end with a question mark, it doesn't belong in the initial interview.** The exceptions to this rule are the brief statements that set up your next question. Bridging comments are this kind of statement, leading into the next WIA ——— TY question:

- *Help me understand.* What's important about ——— to you?
- *I see.* What's important about ——— to you?
- *Hmmm. That's interesting.* What's important about ——— to you?
- ——— *means different things to different people.* What's important about ——— to you?
- *Give me a little more perspective on that.* What's important about ——— to you?
- *Let's assume for a moment that* ——— *has become a reality* for you. What's important about ——— to you?

Use bridging comments to create a smoothly flowing values conversation and avoid sounding like an interrogator.

Go All the Way.

A common mistake for people new to Values-Based Selling is not taking the conversation far enough up the values staircase. This is important because the most meaningful and emotional part of the conversation is toward the top. The farther you go, the better you understand your prospect or client and the more powerful the bond between you.

Your role is to help the client think about what's important. At the top of the values staircase, your client will give you "big picture" values such as these:

- Fulfilling my purpose
- Satisfaction
- Spiritual fulfillment
- Relationship with God
- Happiness
- Feeling good about myself

he VBFP conducts a meaningful conversation about values.
e question, "What's important about money to you?" makes
ople think.

Use the Confirming Question.

As you become more skilled with the values conversation, you'll begin to recognize when you are at or close to the top of the prospect's values staircase.

If you only skimmed the previous sample values conversation, I encourage you to review it now—you may have missed some of its power. Even if you read it carefully, you won't really understand how compelling it is until you conduct the values conversation yourself.

Three common questions about the values conversation are worth focusing on now.

1. **"How long does the values conversation take?"** In the real world, it usually runs five minutes or less per person.

2. **"What happens to a prospect's emotional level during the values conversation?"** In every musical composition there are crescendos, and in every effectively executed values conversation there is an emotional crescendo. The higher you go on the values staircase, the more intense the emotions become. You can tell from some of the words in the sample conversation that Terry's emotional level rose as the conversation progressed. The words he used to describe his values have a special emotional charge for him. Unless you use this values conversation, you will rarely, if ever, see your prospects reach this level of emotion about their financial decisions.

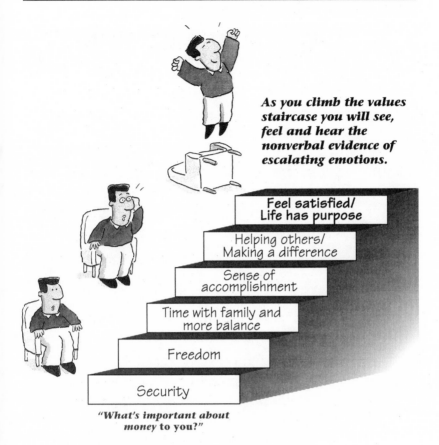

As you climb the values staircase you will see, feel and hear the nonverbal evidence of escalating emotions.

Feel satisfied/
Life has purpose

Helping others/
Making a difference

Sense of
accomplishment

Time with family and
more balance

Freedom

Security

"What's important about money to you?"

3. **"How does this conversation create trust?"** Not only does the values conversation prompt prospects to talk about themselves, but there's a big difference between the superficial chitchat that many financial professionals use to open a client interview and the values conversation. The "big talk" of the values conversation replaces the need for small talk, chitchat, groping for common ground, or talking about your credentials, your experience or your company.

Why Talking About Yourself in the First Five Minutes Is a *Bad* Idea

Do you remember dating?

Can you imagine going on a first date, sitting down with your companion and saying, "I'd like to begin our date by telling you all about . . . me!"?

It would be absurd! And if it's an absurd way to begin a personal relationship, why would anyone think it's an intelligent way to begin a business relationship?

It's not.

What do you think is the best use of your first five minutes with prospective clients?

- Chitchat or small talk about the weather, sports or politics
- Common ground discussions
- You talking about yourself and your company
- Or them talking about their values and what's most important and meaningful to them

Which of these choices is likely to create early feelings of trust, belief that you care about them and desire to do business with you? That's a no-brainer. However, you may find that the biggest challenge of Values-Based Selling isn't learning these powerful strategies, but unlearning some of your old habits. **What got you where you are may not be the best way to get where you want to be.**

Now it's time to consider the specific steps you must take to master the skill of Values-Based Selling. In the next chapter, we'll go through each of the five steps of the values conversation and see how to open effectively, conduct the conversation smoothly, gain precommitment and transition into a complete, honest asset profile or fact finder. There are five steps. You must master them all.

Summary

- Make the most of the first five minutes, and the rest of the interview will be easy.
- The values conversation helps you do the following:
  - ✔ Quickly distinguish Great Clients from the rest of the pack.
  - ✔ Build a high-trust relationship with those Great Clients in five minutes.
  - ✔ Understand fully the values, goals and current financial situation of your clients and prospects.
- The values conversation is easy to learn.
- It is based on the fundamental question, "What's important about money *to you?*"

- You listen a lot more than you talk during the values conversation.

- You use conversational bridging comments to take any awkwardness out of the process.

- You can test whether your prospect is at the top of the values staircase by asking a basic confirming question: "Is there anything more important to you than [*the last value mentioned*]?"

EXERCISE

Practice the values conversation with a friend, family member or existing client. Ask that person, "What's important about money *to you*?" Stop the process when you have confirmed that you are at the top of that person's values staircase. How did the person feel about this process? Did you learn something new about the person?

In this chapter, you've read an example of the values conversation, and you've seen that it builds emotion and creates trust. It is much more effective than needs or wants selling. As you do it in the real world, you will discover how powerful the emotions are. You will feel the bonds of trust develop.

NOTES

_____

_____

_____

_____

_____

_____

_____

_____

_____

_____

_____

_____

_____

_____

_____

_____

_____

_____

_____

3. Master the Values Conversation in Five Easy Steps.

Clearly, you don't open your first meeting by saying, "Hi, I'm Bill. So, uh . . . What's important about money *to you*?" Supporting the simple but meaningful exchange of the values conversation are five easy steps— steps every Values-Based Financial Professional (VBFP) must master to be effective with it.

1. Set the stage.
2. Reset the stage if necessary.
3. Discover core values using the WIA ——— TY questions and bridging comments.
4. Get precommitment to move forward.
5. Transition into total financial discovery and the asset profile or fact finder, and prioritize goals.

There are five easy steps to the values conversation.

How to Set the Stage

Setting the stage is the key to positioning yourself as a trusted advisor rather than a suspect salesperson. It's the most effective way to open the values conversation, superseding and surpassing small talk, chitchat, groping for common ground, and talking about yourself, your credentials, your experience or your company. It paves the way for a smooth values conversation, just as the first few minutes of a well-crafted speech earn the audience's attention and positive reaction.

> There are only two rules for setting the stage:
> 1. Be brief.
> 2. End with, "What's important about money *to you?*

Here's an example of setting the stage, which you'll probably recognize from Chapter 2.

VBFP. I'm glad we were able to get together today, Terry. You've invested time to meet with me, which tells me you must be serious about making smart choices about your money. Is that true?

Terry. Yes, I am.

VBFP. Help me understand. What's important about money *to you?*

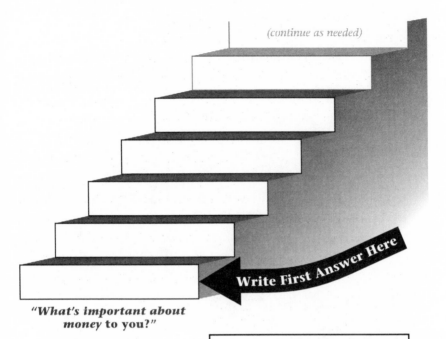

(continue as needed)

Write First Answer Here

"What's important about money to you?"

> *The values conversation always starts with the question: "What's important about money to you?"*

When you have set the stage and you ask the WIA ——— TY question, you are looking for the first answer off the top of the prospect's head—just that first answer, not all the answers. So set the stage with confidence, and then ask "What's important about money *to you?*" with genuine interest. Then shut up, relax and *listen to the answer*. Proceed at your prospect's pace. Remember, this is a conversation, not an interrogation. Setting the stage provides a brief, logical explanation of why you are asking, "What's important about money *to you?*"

Listen and Go at the Prospect's Pace.

Tony Barron was the top agent in the San Diego agency of The Equitable. When he was referred to me for a 21-hour course I taught, Tony began our meeting by explaining all the reasons he didn't think he should take the course. He said, "You know, Bill, I've never taken a class on selling. I don't script things out, I don't memorize responses to objections and I don't have a bunch of canned closes. I've been successful in my 19 years in the business because all I do is listen to my clients and go at their pace."

It was interesting how comfortable Tony felt signing up for my course after I listened to him, went at his pace and helped him discover how enrolling in the course would relate positively to his values. So take Tony's advice: Listen and go at your prospect's pace during the values conversation.

Another way to set the stage will differentiate you from other financial professionals.

VBFP. A lot of people think my job is to sell insurance and investments for meeting specific goals like a secure retirement, funding the children's college education or paying estate taxes. I do that, but my most important function is to help my clients achieve their lifetime financial goals. To be effective, I need to understand the big picture. The key ingredient in all your financial goals is enough money to achieve them. So, help me understand: What's important about money *to you*?

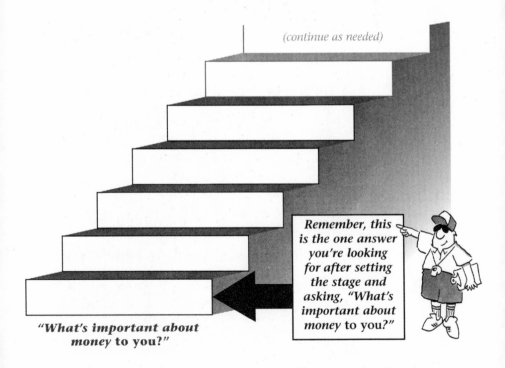

(continue as needed)

Remember, this is the one answer you're looking for after setting the stage and asking, "What's important about money to you?"

"What's important about money to you?"

The more often you set the stage and use the values conversation, the easier the interaction becomes. If you follow the stage-setting formula just as you would a gourmet recipe, the outcome will be equally rewarding. If you take shortcuts or ignore the recipe, you can count on a poor result.

The most important thing to remember in setting the stage is never to change the question. Your stage setting will always end with "What's important about money *to you*?"

The Question—Not!

Never use your product or service in the values question because it almost always leads to a discussion of features instead of the values conversation. Here's what *not* to ask:

What's important about financial planning to you?

What's important about insurance to you?

What's important about investments to you?

What's important about asset allocation to you?

What's important about retirement to you?

What's important about college funding to you?

What's important about a financial advisor to you?

What's important about estate planning to you?

What's important about charity to you?

What's important about this pension plan to you?

The question is "What's important about money *to you?"*

If you specialize in a specific area of financial advice, you can use that specialty in the stage setting and still focus on money. Being client-focused means you focus on what the clients care about and understand. They may not care about or understand what you do, but they care about and understand their money. Here are some simple stage settings to get the conversation on track.

Retirement planning: "The key ingredient to successful retirement planning is having money. With that in mind, help me understand: What's important about money *to you?*"

Estate planning: "People who are concerned with planning their estates have different perspectives about the importance of money. Help me understand: What's important about money *to you?*"

Charitable giving: "People who are interested in charitable endeavors understand that money is not an end in itself. It is a vehicle. Help me understand: What's important about money *to you?*"

Asset management: "People who are concerned about asset management want to make smart choices about their money. Help me understand: What's important about money *to you?*"

Insurance: "Insurance is one vehicle to generate money when you need it. Help me understand: What's important about money *to you?*"

Financial planning: "Financial strategies are only for people like you who are serious about planning their money matters. Help me understand: What's important about money *to you?*"

Pension plans: "I recognize that all the money in this pension isn't yours. But it will help me to understand your perspective about money in order to prepare a proposal about our pension management services. Help me understand: What's important about money *to you?*"

Successful Stage-Setting Techniques From Values-Based Financial Professionals

The samples below provide stage settings successfully used by some top performers. Pay special attention to how each one easily introduces the prospect to the values conversation.

DIAGNOSIS BEFORE PRESCRIPTION

"As a financial professional, I'm always looking for ways to help people like you make smart decisions with their money. I guess I'm a bit like a doctor in that I believe that prescription before diagnosis is malpractice. I find it really helpful to learn as much as possible about you and your needs and objectives. So, [client name], help me understand: What's important about money to you?"

GREG AITKENS
Lincoln Financial
VBFP since 1993

MONEY IS THE COMMON DENOMINATOR.

"Most people meet with me because they are interested in retirement planning, funding their children's education, asset allocation, or handling some other financial issue. The common denominator of all these concerns is money, so let's talk about that first. What's important about money to you?"

CRAIG SNYDER
General Agent,
Allmerica Financial
VBFP since 1992

WHAT WOULD YOU LIKE TO ACCOMPLISH?

"When you think about your investments, there are probably certain things you want to accomplish. I'd like to be able to understand what those things are so I can help you achieve them. So, pertaining to investments, what's important about money to you?"

DENNIS BEEBY
Vice President of Marketing,
Pacific Capital Partners, Inc.
VBFP since 1989

How to Reset the Stage

Most of the time, any one of these methods of setting the stage will engage your prospect in the values conversation by eliciting the anticipated first response. Then you can build on that first response with the subsequent "What's important . . ." questions to continue the values conversation. Sometimes, however, prospects don't understand the first question or simply refuse to answer. Refusal to answer may indicate that you need to reset the stage; it can also be an early warning sign that you are dealing with a difficult person. Which assumption is correct? You won't know until you reset the stage.

Following are ways to reset the stage for people who can't or won't answer your question. For more possible responses to resistance, refer to Appendix C.

Some people just can't answer "What's important about money *to you*?" right off the top of their heads. They need more time to think. They say things like, "I don't know quite how to answer that," "I've never thought about that question before," or "I'm not sure what you mean."

There are also some people who don't want to answer the question. They say things like, "That's a weird question," "Look, I don't want to answer any questions," or "This is my situation; just tell me what you've got."

Trusted advisors have questions they insist be answered. Salespeople just jockey for position so they can make a sale. The skill of resetting the stage will help you deal with those people who can't or won't answer the "What's important about money *to you*?" question right off the bat. Notice it's called "reset the stage"— not "change the question." If you change the question, you eliminate the effectiveness of the values conversation. Never change the question. Reset the stage to stay on purpose.

RESETTING THE STAGE WITH PEOPLE WHO CAN'T ANSWER READILY

To people who may never have considered what's important about money to them, the question might be confusing at first. They honestly don't have an answer. They need more time to think. Resetting the stage buys them that time.

Go ahead and make your prospect more comfortable. Clarify what the question means— but never change the question. The dialogue for resetting the stage may sound like this:

VBFP. *[After setting the stage the first time.]* What's important about money *to you?*

Terry. I am not sure how to answer that.

VBFP. *[Resetting the stage.]* Yes, I understand; it might sound odd at first. I'll bet nobody has ever asked you this before. But please bear with me. In order to help you make smart choices about your money, I need to understand what's important about money *to you.* Think about this very important issue. We'll take as much time as you need. But first, just tell me off the top of your head, what's important about money *to you?*

Resetting the stage validates the prospect's feelings without getting off track. If you back off from your predetermined flow of questions (or, worse yet, you have no predetermined flow of questions), you will appear weak and

Remember never to offer suggestions. You must identify their *values!*

unprofessional. If you get nervous and back off, your prospect will wonder how many other questions you planned to ask that you don't really expect answered. Instead of changing course, use a brief stage resetting to explain why you are asking the question. Reassure the prospect that there is no rush or pressure— and that the answer is crucial.

Then it's time to listen. Let your prospect answer the question. People differ in how long they think before they speak, and you can demonstrate respect with your silence.

RESETTING THE STAGE WITH PEOPLE WHO WON'T ANSWER

What if the prospect doesn't want to answer the question? Some people pride themselves on being difficult. Always maintain a confident posture. You'll either get past their veneer of being difficult and they'll turn out to be wonderful, or you'll get down to the basis of their resistance and find out that they belong in one of the last two categories of clients—Uses You for Information or Doesn't Trust Anybody. No matter what, you win, because your objective is either to engage them in the values conversation or to eliminate an unproductive relationship and move on to someone else.

Consider your current clients. Do any of them make you think, *If I knew then what I know now, I would never have taken this person on as a client?* With the values conversation, you can find out in minutes what otherwise might take months or years to learn: which people you should never do business with in the first place.

If you reset the stage more than once and the prospect is still uncooperative, you probably are dealing with someone who is interested only in using you for information or someone who is incapable of trusting. Politely disengage from these difficult people. Part of becoming a VBFP is quickly disengaging from people who waste your time.

Here's an example of an experience I had with someone who was uncooperative. Resetting the stage dissolved this person's resistance.

Bill. [*After a brief stage setting.*] What's important about money *to you*?

Prospect. [*With a deadly stare, after a protracted silence.*] Well, Mr. Bachrach, you are the financial advisor here. If you don't understand what's important about money, then maybe I'm in the wrong place!

Bill. [*Pausing, then smiling.*] You're absolutely right. I understand what's important about money to me. And I understand what's important about money to all my other clients. However, it would be completely unprofessional for me to give you financial advice until I understand what's important about money *to you*. So, help me understand: What's important about money *to you*?

He considered my response, eventually smiled and answered the question.

Resetting the stage in this case worked effectively because my prospect realized he needed to answer the question so I could help him. He understood that answering would benefit him; it wasn't just information I was trying to gather so I could hammer him with it later in the hope of selling something.

Three Strikes and They're Out!

I advocate the three strikes method.
1. Set the stage.
2. If necessary, reset the stage.
3. If necessary, reset the stage again.

At this point, they're either in or out. If they're uncooperative during this simple exchange, they're giving you a clear signal they won't be cooperative later. Either they are moving into the values conversation by the third stage setting, or you should be walking them to the door.

Be honest with yourself. Prospects who will not cooperate when you ask what's important about money to them are never going to cooperate when it's time to tell you where all their money is. The trusted advisor walks away. The salesperson guts it out to ring the cash register. Yet trusted advisors make lots more money than salespeople.

When you practice resetting the stage, it's important to remember who really benefits. If you follow too much of the old sales training, you might think selling is something you do *to* someone, that it is adversarial and confrontational. But selling done well is not that at all. You're not asking about people's values so you can hammer them with those values when you're trying to close. Instead, you put into perspective the relationship between their values, their goals and their current financial reality. This perspective allows you to help them make better financial choices in order to achieve their goals and, ultimately, fulfill their values.

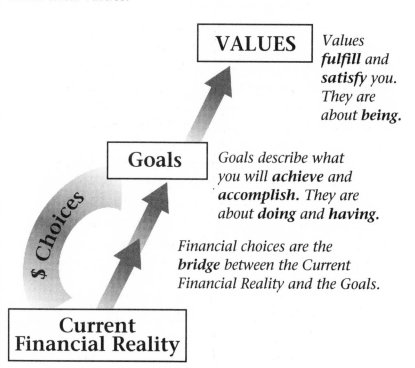

VALUES — *Values* **fulfill** *and* **satisfy** *you. They are about* **being.**

Goals — *Goals describe what you will* **achieve** *and* **accomplish.** *They are about* **doing** *and* **having.**

Financial choices are the **bridge** *between the Current Financial Reality and the Goals.*

Current Financial Reality

How to Discover Core Values in a Conversational Manner

From Chapter 2, you already know how to discover prospects' values by asking each of the WIA ——— TY questions. As you do this, their voices, faces and body language will tell you they're getting emotionally involved. That's good! The higher their emotions rise, the more likely it is they'll trust you. They now have strong emotional reasons that will motivate them to

- answer all the personal financial questions you are going to ask,
- appropriately prioritize financial goals ahead of current wants,
- have confidence in your recommendations,
- implement what you advise them to do,
- refer their friends, relatives and colleagues to you,
- be more responsive to you, their trusted advisor, than to financial products or salespeople, unpredictable events in the market, negative reports from the media or advice from friends.

Don't worry that this information is too personal just because it evokes emotions. Values are meaningful motivators, not private secrets. Remember, you will soon be asking these prospects how much money they make, how much they have and where it is—now, *that's* personal! So you must first earn the right to ask those questions. The values conversation earns you the right.

Use Bridging Comments to Make the Conversation Flow.

Remember to use bridging comments to make the conversation flow. They soften the interview and make it more natural and conversational, and they should be made in a spirit of curiosity. They shouldn't be memorized and recited or put in an arsenal as ammunition for an interrogation. Their sole purpose is to make the conversation comfortable for both you and your clients. Again, here are some examples:

- *"Hmmm, interesting.* What's important about freedom *to you?"*

- *"Security means different things to different people.* What's important about security *to you?"*

- *"Help me understand:* What's important about providing for your family *to you?"*

- *"Give me your perspective.* What's important about making a difference in life *to you?"*

- *"Suppose you are in the position of having accomplished your goals.* What's important about having accomplished those goals *to you?"*

Mastery Tip

Reread the values conversation between the VBFP and Terry in Chapter 2, and notice how the bridging comments were used. It will be apparent to you how these comments make the values questions conversational instead of interrogational so that both the interviewer and the prospect feel comfortable.

How to Get Precommitment

Precommitment begins to establish the basic ground rules of the client/VBFP relationship. It provides evidence that your prospects are serious about their financial future. Precommitment affirms the idea that you and the prospect are establishing a professional *relationship* to help them achieve their financial goals and fulfill their values. Precommitment is not about trapping your prospects or clients into buying something. It's about establishing the rules of the relationship and conveying that you understand what's important to them. Here's a review of precommitment from the values conversation in Chapter 2.

> *Notice how the VBFP uses the prospect's own values in exactly his own words to describe the basis of their professional relationship.*

VBFP. Terry, suppose we can create a strategy that will help you make smart financial choices. I'm talking about the choices you could make to have the *security* and the *freedom* to *spend more time with your family,* to enjoy the *balance* that allows you to feel a great *sense of accomplishment,* and to *make a difference* for other people so you ultimately have the *sense of satisfaction* that your *life has purpose.* If that were the case, would you and I have a basis for working together?

Terry. Absolutely.

VBFP. I think so, too.

Understanding your prospects' values early in the conversation causes the momentum to shift so the prospects want to buy more than you want to sell. It always makes more sense to use your prospect's buying momentum than to apply selling pressure. The shift from passive discussion to buying momentum occurs when prospects discover their emotional reasons (their values) for wanting to take charge of their financial lives. The connection between smart financial decisions and core values builds the buying momentum.

If their answer to the precommitment question is yes, you have established an agreement in principle between you and your new clients.

How you ask this question is more important than the question itself. If you are concerned that your prospect might be put off, it probably has more to do with your fear of sounding too "salesy." **Ask with curiosity and sincerity.** Don't make it sound like a hammer close. Great Clients will not be offended when you politely confirm that you are both on the right track to helping them get what is important to them.

Financial professionals who don't ask for precommitment are like gamblers who don't know the rules before they bet. Would you bet on a football game with someone who refused to tell you the amount of the bet or the point spread? Of course not. You wouldn't even play a simple game without knowing the rules. And this isn't a game. It's your business; it's your career. So, if you must know the rules before you play a game, how much more important is it to know the rules when dealing with the future of your career?

Yet how many times have you seen financial professionals who invest an incredible amount of time preparing strategies and proposals for people who haven't told them under what conditions they would do business? The gambler who doesn't clarify the rules loses some money, but the cost to the financial professional who proceeds without laying the groundwork can be a frustrating and mediocre career.

It amazes me to hear financial professionals who berate their prospects and clients for not taking action. I always wonder, Did these prospects ever agree to take any action or make any commitments? Did the prospects ever say, "When you bring me a plan like this, that's what I'll implement," or is there just an expectation based on a fantasy about what should happen after all the work has been done to prepare a strategy? What were the rules? *Did anybody lay down the rules in the first place?*

When clients or prospects don't understand the rules, it's unreasonable to expect them to play by those rules. If you don't establish what the rules are before you go to work for that prospect, then you have no one to blame but yourself when someone doesn't act on your advice. Get precommitment *before* you go to work—and save lots of time. Who does business this way? *Professionals* do.

How to Transition into Total Financial Discovery

The values conversation gives the financial professional an intimate understanding of the emotional motives of the prospects—motives that can solidify their drive to take charge of their financial lives. The bond of trust between the financial professional and the prospects causes prospects to accept the financial professional's help.

When a financial professional earns the prospects' trust and creates compelling emotions about their future, then a business relationship will be established. If not, no business is likely to happen. If you have sometimes had difficulty getting your prospects to tell you where all their money was, you probably failed to achieve one of these primary objectives first.

Positive Emotions + Trust = Buying Momentum
Buying momentum means that prospects want to buy more than you want to sell.

For you to help your prospects, next you must know where all the money is. You cannot do your best work otherwise; in fact, you may unintentionally mislead your client with bad advice if you don't have complete information.

Fortunate for both you and your prospects, feelings of trust inspire prospects to truthfully answer your questions about their assets.

To obtain complete information about your prospects' finances, you will embark on the process of total financial discovery. Here's one way to make the transition from the values conversation to total financial discovery (again, using the values conversation from Chapter 2):

> **VBFP.** Now that we understand what's important to you, the next steps are to clarify your current financial situation fully and to prioritize your financial goals accurately. Which one would you like to do first?

> **Terry.** Let's start with my goals. The two things I am very concerned about right now are having enough money to help my kids with college and being able to retire by the time I'm about 60.

Here's another effective way to make this important transition:

> **VBFP.** Now that we understand what's important to you, the next steps are to be absolutely clear about your current financial situation and to prioritize your financial goals. Tell me about your goals.

Essentially, you are now making the transition into your fact finder or asset profile system.

Now it's time for you to practice. The next chapter will lead you through your first few values conversations and start you on the road to becoming a full-fledged VBFP.

Summary

- The values conversation can be broken down into five steps:

  1. Set the stage.

  2. Reset the stage (necessary only if the person can't or won't respond to the WIA ——— TY question immediately).

  3. Discover core values. (Conduct the values conversation.)

  4. Get precommitment.

  5. Transition into total financial discovery.

- Three strikes and they're out: Give the prospect a reasonable number of chances to cooperate before disengaging. If you've set the stage once and reset it twice without successfully obtaining cooperation, show that prospect to the door.

- Positive Emotions + Trust = Buying Momentum

EXERCISE 1

Review the stage settings modeled on pages 52 and 53; these are used successfully by some top performers. Now, write one or two ways you might set the stage for your values conversation. These can be very similar to any you have read so far in this book. Choose words, phrases, and sentences that are comfortable for you, but remember the following:

- Be brief.

- Explain the reason for asking the WIA ——— TY question.

- End by asking, "What's important about money *to you?*"

Read aloud the one or two possible stage settings you've written until you feel very comfortable saying them. Decide which one you will try first when you practice the values conversation in the next chapter.

EXERCISE 2

Review the values conversation between the VBFP and Terry in Chapter 2. In the margin, identify each section of the values conversation: stage setting, discovering core values, using bridging comments, getting precommitment and transitioning into total financial discovery.

NOTES

4. Action! See the Benefits of the Values Conversation for Yourself.

The payoff from everything you learn in this book depends on how good you become at eliciting compelling emotions and earning trust through effective execution of the values conversation. Once you begin applying what you've learned so far, the light goes on: It all makes complete sense.

A Values-Based Financial Professional (VBFP) is neither someone who simply sells financial products and services to help people meet their goals nor someone who matches products to client needs. He or she is someone who

- creates high-trust, values-based relationships with clients rather than transaction-based "one-night stands";
- becomes a valuable, trusted resource for clients;
- helps clients create a strategy not only to meet their goals but ultimately to fulfill their values in life;
- has much more impact on clients than an investment salesperson, insurance agent or financial product salesperson.

The choice you make now about whether or not to practice the values conversation will have a dramatic impact on your future, regardless of the current level of your success. The rest of the book won't make much sense until you've had personal experience with the values conversation, so now is the right time to start practicing what you have learned so far. This is a skills book; therefore, you must apply the skills as you go to get value from it.

No matter who you choose to practice with, be sure to 1) set the stage for the values conversation with a few introductory sentences that end with, "What's important about money to you?" and 2) use bridging comments before the WIA —— TY questions to facilitate the flow of the conversation. ("Hmmm. That's interesting." "Give me some perspective on that." "—— means different things to different people.")

You can begin practicing right away with existing clients, friends, and new prospects. Here's how to handle each situation.

Practice with Existing Clients.

Call your three best clients and conduct the values conversation with them over the phone. It will enhance your relationship and give you the practice you need to master Values-Based Selling. All you have to do before the call is write down the brief stage-setting sentences you wish to use. On the phone, you can read the stage setting rather than try to say it from memory, and it still works as effectively as a face-to-face values conversation. Try this for openers:

> **VBFP.** I am always looking for ways to serve my clients better. I'm reading a book that describes the value of asking what's important about money to you. I know a lot about you, but we've never had this particular conversation. Since it will focus our work together on your top priorities, I think it's important. Help me understand: What's important about money *to you*?

Then be quiet and wait for an answer. Turn to one of the blank values staircases on pages 78–86, and write the answer in the first step at the bottom. Then ask, "What's important about ——— to you?" You can use bridging comments, but *never change* the WIA ——— TY question. There are a few bridging comments next to the values staircase to use during your practice conversations.

Mastery Tip

If you feel uncomfortable introducing the conversation, you can take the pressure off by telling your client, "I've never done this before. I am calling you because you're one of my best clients, so maybe we can just give this a shot together. Please bear with me if I seem a little awkward; I think we'll both find this conversation very enlightening. What's important about money *to you?"*

Practice With Friends.

Call three friends who think money is important. Here's how to set the stage with a friend.

> **VBFP.** I've just learned something new that I think will help me better understand my clients and build my business. I'd like to practice it with you before I integrate it into my client interview. Do you have five or ten minutes to help me out?
>
> ***Friend.*** Sure.
>
> **VBFP.** Great. I know money is important to you, so how would you answer this question: What's important about money *to you?*

If your friends give you any grief (they sometimes do that), just say this:

VBFP.   Listen, I'm serious here. I need some practice with this, and you're my friend. I know money is important to you. Go along with me and answer this question honestly: What's important about money *to you*?

Practice With Prospects.

There is nothing about this conversation that can hurt your relationship with a new prospect. Whether you conduct it fantastically well the first time or just obtain a few answers from the prospect, you're better off than if you hadn't asked the WIA ——— TY question at all.

Use the values staircase to remind you of the process and to write down the prospect's answers as they are given.

Action=Results!

Practice, Practice, Practice!

Mastery is "the mysterious process during which what is at first difficult becomes progressively easier and more pleasurable through practice," said George Leonard in his book, *Mastery*. The more you use the values conversation, the easier and more pleasurable it becomes. If you follow the steps of the values conversation carefully, your outcome will become easy, pleasurable and rewarding.

Remember, you are reading this book to develop your skills. So start developing them now. Remember not to lead or interrupt. The higher your prospects go up the staircase, the more time they may take to reflect on their answers—so much the better. Notice the emotion. Your job is to do the following (in roughly this order):

1. Ask.
2. Listen.
3. Ask.
4. Empathize and listen.
5. Ask.
6. Relax and listen some more.
7. Ask.
8. Listen some more.
9. Remember: listen and proceed at their pace.

Go ahead: Put the book down now, and give it a try. This book won't go anywhere while you are practicing. If you want, first read the dialogue given in Chapter 2 again, then practice the values conversation. The rest of what you learn will make a lot more sense if you have a little experience in conducting this meaningful conversation.

Practice, practice, practice. Harvey Mackay wrote in *Swim With the Sharks Without Being Eaten Alive*, "It isn't practice that makes perfect. You have to add one word. It's perfect practice that makes perfect. . . . [Otherwise,] you're only perfecting an error." You can't control the outcome of the values conversation, so you don't know whether the result will be perfect. But you can control what you do, how you ask the questions, how you perfectly set the stage, how you perfectly use bridging comments and whether you pay attention and listen. You can control perfect execution from your side of the values conversation, and that will dramatically affect the result. So, focus on your side of the values conversation and practice that perfectly.

Go ahead; practice right now.

Practice 1

> *"We can't cross a bridge until we come to it, but I always like to lay down a pontoon ahead of time."*
>
> BERNARD BARUCH

(continue as needed)

Write First Answer Here

"What's important about money to you?"

Bridging Comments

"——— means different things to different people. WIA ——— TY?"

"Hmmm, that's interesting. WIA ——— TY?"

"Give me some more perspective on that. WIA ——— TY?"

Practice 2

> *"World-class achievers in sports and business are not admired while they are practicing. The results of an incredible amount of practice earn admiration."*
>
> BILL BACHRACH

(continue as needed)

Write First Answer Here

"What's important about money to you?"

Bridging Comments

"———— means different things to different people. WIA ———— TY?"

"Hmmm, that's interesting. WIA ———— TY?"

"Give me some more perspective on that. WIA ———— TY?"

Practice 3

Mark Twain claimed that it took him two weeks to prepare an impromptu speech.

(continue as needed)

Write First Answer Here

"What's important about money to you?"

Bridging Comments

"———— means different things to different people. WIA ———— TY?"

"Hmmm, that's interesting. WIA ———— TY?"

"Give me some more perspective on that. WIA ———— TY?"

Practice 4

> *"Before everything else, getting ready is the secret of success."*
>
> HENRY FORD

(continue as needed)

Write First Answer Here

"What's important about money to you?"

Bridging Comments

"———— means different things to different people. WIA ———— TY?"

"Hmmm, that's interesting. WIA ———— TY?"

"Give me some more perspective on that. WIA ———— TY?"

Practice 5

> *"If you don't do your homework, you won't make your free throws."*
>
> LARRY BIRD

(continue as needed)

Write First Answer Here

"What's important about money to you?"

Bridging Comments

"———— means different things to different people. WIA ———— TY?"

"Hmmm, that's interesting. WIA ———— TY?"

"Give me some more perspective on that. WIA ———— TY?"

Practice 6

> ### "Good fortune is what happens when opportunity meets with preparation."
> THOMAS EDISON

(continue as needed)

Write First Answer Here

"What's important about money to you?"

Bridging Comments

*"———— means different things to different people.
WIA ———— TY?"*

"Hmmm, that's interesting. WIA ———— TY?"

"Give me some more perspective on that. WIA ———— TY?"

Practice 7

"For all your days prepare,
And meet them ever alike;
When you are the anvil, bear;
When you are the hammer, strike."

EDWARD MARKHAM

(continue as needed)

Write First Answer Here

"What's important about
money to you?"

Bridging Comments

"——— means different things to different people.
WIA ——— TY?"

"Hmmm, that's interesting. WIA ——— TY?"

"Give me some more perspective on that. WIA ——— TY?"

Practice 8

> ## *"The secret of success is to be ready for opportunity when it comes."*
> ### BENJAMIN DISRAELI

(continue as needed)

Write First Answer Here

"What's important about money to you?"

Bridging Comments

"———— means different things to different people. WIA ———— TY?"

"Hmmm, that's interesting. WIA ———— TY?"

"Give me some more perspective on that. WIA ———— TY?"

Practice 9

> *"The future belongs to those who prepare for it."*
>
> RALPH WALDO EMERSON

(continue as needed)

Write First Answer Here

"What's important about money to you?"

Bridging Comments

"——— *means different things to different people.*
WIA ——— *TY?"*

"Hmmm, that's interesting. WIA ——— *TY?"*

"Give me some more perspective on that. WIA ——— *TY?"*

How Did It Go?

Congratulations! You have now taken the first step toward mastering the values conversation. In the next two weeks, do whatever it takes to get another 20 or so real experiences with "What's important about money to you?" Soon you will possess this skill as your own.

The first time you try anything new, you may feel a little awkward. That's OK. It's just part of the learning, growing and improvement process. Look at it this way: If it were perfectly comfortable the first time, everyone would do it. Then people like you and me who are serious about our success wouldn't have a competitive edge.

I'm sure you noticed the emotional response of the people you had the values conversation with. Some of them probably had to think about the questions a few moments to come up with their answers. I'll bet it was challenging to be quiet after asking the WIA ——— TY question and to resist helping them out and putting words in their mouths. The secret is to remember to respect people enough to let them come up with their own answers. People buy to fulfill *their* values, not yours.

Good Things Happen for People Who Implement New Ideas Right Away.

Jim Paxton, a sales manager and producer with John Hancock, listened intently to my presentation at his President's Club conference. He couldn't wait for the opportunity to try this stuff out. On his flight home, he struck up a conversation with the man in the seat next to him. As Jim told his new acquaintance what he did for a living, he thought, Nothing ventured, nothing gained. Instead of saying that he sold life insurance and securities, he said, "I help people make smart choices about money." Then he asked, "What's important about money *to you?*"

The rest is history. "The values conversation worked wonders!" Jim reported. "We laid tremendous groundwork to do business together, even though he lives in San Diego and I live in Washington State. He has since placed his life insurance business with me, generating a $9,000 commission!"

Jim calls the values conversation "the underlying key to my success." Not too long ago, Jim was in San Diego playing golf with this new client and two of the client's friends. The client thought Jim should meet these millionnaire friends so he could help them make smart choices about their money, too.

Be like Jim. Go for it. You are wasting your time if you read this book but never implement what you learn. *Values-Based Selling* can show you the way to a higher level of success, but the book alone won't take you there. You take yourself by practicing and applying what you learn.

Harness Don Shula's Concept of *Overlearning.*

Legendary coach Don Shula says,

Overlearning means that the players are so prepared for the game that they have the skill and confidence needed to make the big play. More than anything else, overlearning— constant practice, constant attention to getting the details right every time— produces hunger to be in the middle of the action. When players have absolutely no doubt about what they're supposed to do or how to do it, they thrive on pressure. If the heat's on, they want it coming their way. If the player is a halfback, he wants the ball. If he's an end, he wants the pass thrown to him. If he's a lineman, he wants to make the important block or tackle.

Overlearning for financial professionals means they want to be in the action, talking to prospects, conducting client interviews, asking for referrals, creating financial strategies, coaching clients on implementing financial strategies—*doing business instead of sitting on the sidelines.*

Overlearning for you will mean a commitment to memorize an effective stage setting, to be brilliant at resetting the stage when necessary, to become comfortable with bridging comments and moving people through the values conversation, to be confident and gain precommitment, and to transition smoothly into the fact finder or asset profile. Overlearning will make Values-Based Selling second nature to you.

Values Conversation Do's and Don'ts

During almost a decade of practicing, perfecting and teaching the values conversation, I have experienced and observed the most common mistakes made as people become VBFPs or fail to do so. To avoid these mistakes, carefully read the following table of do's and don'ts. By following the strategy it sets forth, you can quickly master the values conversation.

Do follow the recipe. The WIA ——— TY question is what gets values responses.

Don't rephrase the question. A different question will produce a nonvalues response. The values conversation doesn't work without the WIA ——— TY questions.

Do focus your first meeting on "What's important about money to you?"

Don't start by building a little rapport before asking the WIA ——— TY question. The WIA ——— TY questions build trust, which is more important than rapport.

Do be quiet and listen to your prospect's core values.

Don't think you must disclose your core values to prospects before the prospects will disclose their core values to you.

Do use the prospect's exact words to fill in the WIA ——— TY staircase.

Don't change prospects' words. Never paraphrase.

Do proceed at your prospects' pace, and allow time for them to think.

Don't rush the values conversation.

Values Conversation Do's And Don'ts

Do accept your prospects' values without judgment or comments.

Don't project your own values onto prospects.

Do appreciate and enjoy prospects' emotional response.

Don't discourage people from being emotional.

Do pay close attention to prospects during this conversation. Demonstrate that you care.

Don't be casual about the values conversation— your prospect may think you don't care.

Do allow the values conversation to go on as long as necessary until the prospects acknowledge they have reached the top of their core values staircase.

Don't stop too soon, before prospects have reached their highest core values.

Do use bridging comments to be conversational.

Don't interrogate.

Do wait during silences until the prospects respond.

Don't put words in a prospect's mouth.

Do write down prospects' values. Writing down their answers provides a powerful visual connection for them and shows that you care enough to record their answers.

Don't rely on your memory.

Do adopt Values-Based Selling as a philosophy and a way of doing business to help people fulfill their values.

Don't employ this technique to manipulate your clients' emotions so that you can get them to buy.

The values conversation is all about listening.

Mastery Tip

Circle or put a check mark by those do's and don'ts you think might be challenging for you. Then, as you practice, give yourself credit for improving in those areas!

In Part One of this book, you've seen how to lay a solid foundation—working with Great Clients, deliberately building trust in the first five minutes, completing the values conversation and putting all that you know into action. Now its time to get to work on creating a financial strategy that meets your client's values.

Summary

- You must practice the values conversation to benefit from it.
- Changing old habits is always difficult, but changing from your old interview style to the values conversation is well worth the challenge.
- The values conversation requires attentive listening.
- The values conversation is about discovering your clients' values—not about disclosing your own.
- Keep practicing!

EXERCISE

Follow the Mastery Tip on page 91. Make several copies of your marked-up table of do's and don'ts. Every time you practice the values conversation, rate yourself on how well you did in overcoming the challenges you checked.

NOTES

_____

_____

_____

_____

_____

_____

_____

_____

_____

_____

_____

_____

_____

_____

_____

_____

_____

_____

_____

_____

_____

PART II

Once You've Laid a
Foundation
of Trust,
Building
Your Clients'
Financial
Future Is
a Snap.

5. Get Complete Financial Disclosure in the First Meeting.

Face it: Without trust, nobody is going to tell you where all the money is. Once you have created trust by using the values conversation, you can move easily into the discovery part of the interview. This will naturally lead to seeking and obtaining prospects' commitment to take charge of their financial future. The values conversation dovetails with any fact finder or asset-profile system. Managed properly, it positions you for a direct, open, honest and thorough discovery experience. Regardless of which data gathering tools you use, the objective is always the same: **Discover all the assets and prioritize goals.**

You plot this factual information on a Financial Road Map along with the values. (See pages 110 and 111 for an example.) This compelling visual picture of the clients' lives makes it extremely clear where they are now, where they want to be, and what's important about working to get there.

What Is Discovery?

Discovery allows you to put the truth on paper, where your clients can look at and consider it. They can then decide what they like about their financial truth and what they want to change. This positions you to help them create the new reality they desire. The financial professional puts on paper the prospects' values, the current reality of their financial situation and their financial goals. This truth can be a wake-up call to get them to act. Nothing motivates like the truth: It stirs emotions and inspires commitment.

Discovery allows the financial professional to clarify the relationship between values, the current situation and tangible goals.

When faced with their financial reality some people will think, "Boy, I am on track. Everything is cool. Things are going well." In these cases, the financial professional should negotiate a relationship to help the prospect stay on track. Use words like *accelerate, optimal, coaching, accountability,* and *implement.*

Other people will examine their financial reality and realize, "Hey, I'm really not on track. I'd better get my stuff together!" This provides the impetus for them to hire you to create an effective financial strategy and to act as coach to help implement it.

Skillfully guided, the whole discovery process takes less than one hour, provided the prospect does almost all the talking.

Do not listen to the naysayers who claim that people won't tell you where all their money is during the first interview. If you get good enough, your prospects will tell you everything you need and want to know because they trust you with the information.

Trust does not depend on the amount of time two people have known each other; trust depends on the depth of understanding that develops and the events that occur between them. The values conversation is a deliberate trust-building event. It puts you in the position of having earned the right to discuss in detail the clients' financial goals and current financial situation.

The Goal of Discovery

Just as the values conversation is the key to gaining prospects' trust, discovery is the key to having the information you need to create a compelling financial strategy. The eight objectives of discovery are as follows:

1. **Establish financial goals.** Ascertain prospects' tangible wants and desires (e.g., retirement, financial independence, college, a special trip or celebration, a vacation home, a charitable endeavor, estate preservation).

2. **Use a Financial Road Map to illustrate the gap between where your prospects are now and where they want to be.** (A detailed explanation of the Financial Road Map begins on page 102.) Once their goals have been established, you can refer to them as "personal milestones."

3. **Discover all facts about prospects' current financial situation.** Use financial documents to confirm the facts.

4. **Chart/plot on the Financial Road Map what you've discovered.**

5. Get commitment from prospects to the process of creating a financial strategy.

6. Disengage from prospects who do not, cannot or will not commit.

7. Discuss the services you'll provide (and the cost).

8. Set an appointment to present your recommended financial strategy.

Remember to use values rather than goals to motivate. Goals provide tangible targets, but values provide the emotional pull that motivates people to act—values are like an emotional magnet.

Product Salesperson or Values-Based Financial Professional?

Unfortunately, some so-called financial professionals use the fact finder as a tool for simply selling predetermined products. A few fact finders are extremely product-leading, and in some hands they are blatantly manipulative. An effective asset profile or fact-finder experience is meant to be a service to clients to help them make intelligent choices about their money. It should not be a search for hot buttons so predetermined products can be sold.

Instead of manipulating clients this way, consider yourself a "life advisor" who specializes in money. Because you have earned your prospects' trust prior to the discovery part of the interview, you can eliminate the questions designed to disturb your prospects or set them up for a product sale. This will shorten the interview time and increase its effectiveness.

When you are trusted to help your clients create a clear vision of their future benchmarked against their present, they will buy all the products and financial services they need without coercion from you. They want to buy more than you want to sell.

The Eight Steps of Discovery

1. ESTABLISH FINANCIAL GOALS.

In Chapter 2, the Values-Based Financial Professional (VBFP) ended the values conversation with a transition to discovery. This is a spoken transition in which you mention the core values the prospect has revealed and tie those values to the discovery questions. You can ask, as the VBFP did in the sample values conversation, whether prospects wish to talk first about goals or their financial situation. If you do that, be prepared to start with either one. Here's how to transition into financial goals:

> **VBFP.** Now that we are clear about what's important to you, the next step is to align your financial goals with what you have shared with me so far. What goals do you have that require money to achieve?

2. DEVELOP A FINANCIAL ROAD MAP.

A great way to help your prospects visualize their financial future is to draw them a Financial Road Map illustrating their goals as milestones along the way to arriving at their ultimate destination, their values. The Financial Road Map is a visual summary of the detailed information you gather. Compile it from your confidential questionnaire, fact finder, asset profile or whatever tool you employ during the initial interview. This perspective on their lives—past, present and future—will inspire people to take charge of their financial well-being much more effectively than will sales techniques and education about financial products and issues.

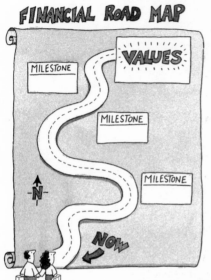

As prospects indicate the goals they have that require money, write each on the Financial Road Map. Write them in chronological order along the road toward their values. By putting prospects' lives on paper, you demonstrate the emotional relationship between their financial choices and a fulfilling, satisfying life. You set each financial goal on the Financial Road Map as a personal milestone for your clients.

Two components of this visual aid are now in place: the intangible emotional motives that will drive them to execute their strategy (their values) and their tangible financial goals. Now it is time to calculate where they are financially today.

This illustration shows the clients' goals (milestones) and values (what's important) plotted on a Financial Road Map. To view the entire road map, see pages 110 and 111.

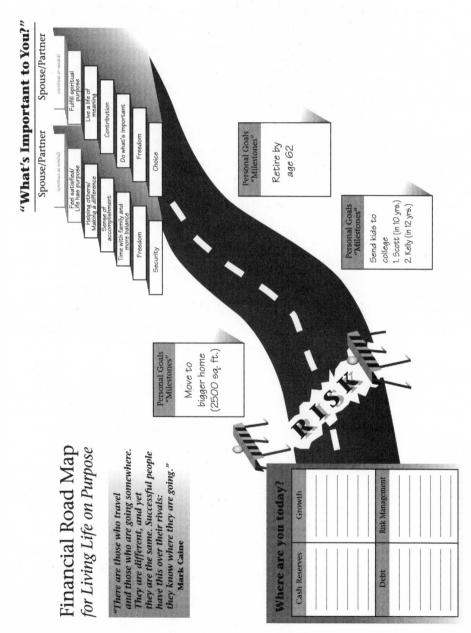

3. TRANSITION INTO FINANCIAL FACTS.

Before you start the fact-finding portion of the interview, remind yourself how sensitive this conversation can be for prospects: For some people it is a very personal experience to reveal where all their money is. That's why, in Values-Based Selling, we create trust before asking these questions.

Consider these statistics from a study conducted by *Worth* magazine (June 1994) and Roper/Starch Worldwide, one of the country's largest market research firms:

> *It's not surprising that as money opens fears, it closes mouths. Among 80 touchy subjects we brought up, money was the one Americans said they feel the least comfortable discussing, well ahead of religion and politics, topics once considered taboo. While 58% say their spouse knows how much they make, just 15% say their best friend knows their income.*

On the one hand it's important to be sensitive to clients' feelings about their money. But it's equally important to be direct and confident when asking where all their assets are, because you can't do your job professionally and effectively without this information. Your mission is to be skilled enough to comfortably facilitate this conversation.

The trust gained through the values conversation gives the VBFP an advantage in obtaining full financial disclosure. Moreover, the effective VBFP insists that prospects bring all their financial documents with them to this first meeting. Using documents to confirm the facts makes sense for at least three reasons.

1. Most people cannot accurately remember every dime of their assets.

2. What people think they own and what they actually own often differ.

3. Your comfort and familiarity with handling their documents reinforces their trust in you and confirms their belief that you are a competent financial professional.

Here's one way to move gracefully into the phase of discovering the prospect's current financial situation.

> **VBFP.** Our next step is to have a thorough, honest, confidential discussion about your present financial situation. Let's have a look at your financial papers and documents, and then we can discuss where you are now.

Ask about everything, including the following:

- Income: both spouses (tax returns)
- Retirement plans: company, 401(k), Keogh, SEP, IRA, RRSP, TSA, other (statements)
- Savings accounts: bank accounts, money market funds (statements)
- CDs (statements)
- Brokerage accounts: stocks, bonds, mutual funds (statements)
- Insurance: life, disability, annuities (policies/contracts)
- Real estate: residence, vacation ownership, investment property (appraisals, loan information, statements)
- Precious metals, art and collectibles (current market values, appraisals)

- Business: owners' balance sheets, profit-and-loss statements (current and previous four years, buy-out agreements)
- Expected inheritance

As you read through the direct evidence provided by the prospect, transfer the bottom line of each asset onto a confidential questionnaire.

Four Quadrants of the Current Financial Situation

1. **Cash Reserves**—Cash reserves are saved for an emergency and future comfort, equal to 30–180 days of expenses.

2. **Debt-Elimination Strategy**—Debt is the enemy of growth and net worth. There are a few legitimate reasons to use debt as leverage. However, when you ask most people how much debt they would like to have, "Zero!" is the common answer. Create a debt-elimination strategy for your clients. It's good business. It's the right thing to do.

3. **Risk Management**—The risks of life cannot be wished away. Insurance is the best vehicle to mitigate risks—health insurance, car insurance, homeowner's insurance, various liability insurances, disability insurance, life insurance, long-term care insurance, insurance to fund buy/sell agreements or estate taxes. You don't have to attend to each of these areas personally. Perhaps you prefer to have a strategic alliance with someone you trust who can serve your client's needs.

"Where are you today?"

Cash Reserves		Growth Strategy	
Where are you now?	Where do you want to be?	Where are you now?	Where do you want to be?
Action: _____ **Objective:** • Prepared for emergency • Save for big purchases *in advance* *Benefit/Why do it?* ★ It feels good! Once built, the deposit goes toward growth.		**Action:** _____ **Objective:** • Achieve goals/milestones *Benefit/Why do it?* ★ It feels good! This is the money that achieves your goals! Lifetime strategy of 8–12% average annual return over time	
Debt		Risk Management Insurance	
Where are you now?	Where do you want to be?	Where are you now?	Where do you want to be?
Action: _____ **Objective:** • Debt reduction/elimination • Eliminate enemy of growth • No upstream swimming *Benefit/Why do it?* ★ It feels good! Once reduced or eliminated, the payment goes toward growth.		**Action:** _____ **Objective:** • Mitigate impact and reduce risk of unpleasant events • Block negative consequences of events that could prevent financial strategy from unfolding and creating the life we want *Benefit/Why do it?* ★ It feels good! ★ It's prudent.	

"Imagine what life will be like when . . . "
- you have a prudent amount of cash reserves
- your debt is gone
- your risks are completely mitigated
- your growth strategy is flourishing/moving you toward your goals

"Give me some words . . ."

"Imagine how you would feel . . . "

As a VBFP, it is incumbent on you to be sure these areas of risk are covered. It's not prudent to have a great financial growth strategy and leave your client exposed to singular events that can wipe it out. (I think this area is fertile ground for future lawsuits. Imagine the complaint: "You held yourself out as a financial professional, yet you never mentioned I was under-insured!")

4. **Growth**—Asset growth bridges the gap between the current financial situation and the goals. Assets that are appreciating in value can be accessed to fund future financial goals. This is the part everyone likes best.

In the beginning of some client relationships, money will flow regularly into the debt reduction and cash reserve strategy. The purpose of insurance, cash reserves and debt elimination is to facilitate an obstacle-free flow of money into asset growth and wealth accumulation so goals are achieved and values fulfilled. Eventually, when cash reserves reach the target and debt is eliminated, the revenue that was going into those areas can be redirected to flow into the growth pool. Many insurance premiums are ongoing payments for life, others "vanish" and some, like disability, are only important until a client is financially independent. Insurance premiums that cease at some point will mean more revenue that can be channeled into the growth quadrant. Accumulation in some insurance policies can be part of the growth strategy.

All your future work with a client will be based on the information you gather in this interview: the person's values, goals and current financial situation. **You can be effective only to the degree that you have gathered complete, accurate information.** To confirm that your information is complete, make a statement something like this:

VBFP. This conversation has been very helpful. The strategy I present to you will be only as accurate as the information you have given me today. Keeping in mind that everything we discuss is totally confidential, is there anything you have not yet shared with me regarding your assets and financial situation?

Or ask your client:

VBFP. Is there anything else you can think of that I should know in order to develop a comprehensive and accurate financial strategy for you?

VALUES-BASED FINANCIAL PROFESSIONALS GATHER MORE ASSETS.

"Your program is excellent, interesting, unique and practical! I have found it to be financially rewarding already. The first time I used the values conversation with an existing client, I uncovered over $500,000 in assets I didn't know about. I believe your approach quickly develops trust with prospects and existing clients in a simple and nonthreatening way."

DAVID FERRIE
Vice President, Nesbitt Burns

Financial Road Map®
for Living Life on Purpose

"There are those who travel
and those who are going somewhere.
They are different, and yet
they are the same. Successful people
have this over their rivals:
they know where they are going."
Mark Caine

Personal Goals
"Milestones"

Move to
bigger home
(2500 sq. ft.)

Where are you today?

Cash Reserves		Growth	
Now	**To Be**	**Now**	**To Be**
$14,000 2 mo. living expenses	$28,000 4 mo. living expenses	(Fill in with current amounts)	(Fill in with target amounts)
Action: $500/month for 28 months		**Action:** Max out Qual. $ $ Into Equity Vehicles $ Into Fixed Vehicles	

Debt		Risk Management	
Now	**To Be**	**Now**	**To Be**
$9,000 unsecured $200,000 mortgage	$0 unsecured Pay on current mortgage schedule	Disability Health Liability Life Funded Buy/sell 2nd to die	Protected to finance events that could reduce or eliminate cash reserves, growth funds, or incur debt
Action: $1,000/month for 9 months		**Action:** Insurance review and increase as necessary	

"What's Important to You?"

Spouse/Partner   Spouse/Partner

(continue as needed)	(continue as needed)
Feel satisfied/ Life has purpose	Fulfill spiritual purpose
Helping others/ Making a difference	Live a life of meaning
Sense of accomplishment	Contribution
Time with family and more balance	Do what's important
Freedom	Freedom
Security	Choice

Personal Goals "Milestones"

Retire by
age 62

Personal Goals "Milestones"

Send kids to
college
1. Scott (in 10 yrs.)
2. Kelly (in 12 yrs.)

**To receive a free sample of a blank Financial Road Map by mail,
fax your address and request to Bachrach & Associates, Inc.
at (619) 558-0748, or e-mail us at info@bachrachvbs.com.**
This printed document cannot be faxed or e-mailed to you.

4. CHART/PLOT ON THE FINANCIAL ROAD MAP WHAT YOU'VE DISCOVERED.

To create a compelling visual representation of the information you have discovered, write the information on the client's personal Financial Road Map. The result should be a visual and emotional representation of the present and future, offering the client perspective and showing the relationship between current choices and their eventual consequences.

5. GET COMMITMENT.

Some clients may become introspective as they see their lives on a Financial Road Map. This is good. They are clarifying the future they say they want: *their* goals in *their* time frame to ultimately fulfill *their* values. In the short time you have spent together, a bright, compelling future has been laid out for them, and their past and present are clear and inarguable (the truth is the truth). The systematic process you have taken them through may seem almost magical. Never have they seen their future so clearly. Never have their choices seemed so simple. Never have they trusted a financial professional so much.

Yet you have done zero selling. They may well ask at this point, "Can you help us with this?" They feel extremely compelled to take action, but they should feel no pressure from you.

This remarkably strong relationship has been built in an incredibly short time. It happened because you asked specific, effective questions. You avoided common

sales jargon. You had enough respect to listen attentively, and you recorded and presented information powerfully so your clients would be motivated to take action. It happened because you are confident that you know how to lead your clients down the path of financial success. Your clients trust you in part because you trust yourself.

You've laid a strong foundation, and now it's time for your prospects to make some commitments. Before you go to work for them, they must agree to do four things:

1. Hire you to create a strategy to bridge the gap between where they are now and where they want to be.

2. Implement that strategy immediately in order to create the financial reality they desire.

3. Adjust their spending habits, if necessary, to make their plan come true.

4. Make future investments and buy insurance contracts, as appropriate.

Here are two examples of how to ask for commitments, depending on how you get paid for your services (fee or no fee).

VBFP. Now that I understand what's important to you and we've seen the gap between where you are now and where you want to be, I can help you develop a plan. First, I need to get a check from you for $——— as a deposit against the final cost of the plan. Make the check out to ———. I'll get started right away to put together a strategy for you.

VBFP. I appreciate the completeness and the honesty of your answers. I don't charge for the up-front work of creating your financial strategy. I get paid when you decide you like the strategy I've created and you implement it. Before I start working on a plan for you, I really need to know if you are truly serious about imple- menting a strategy that will bridge the gap between where you are now and where you want to be. Are you ready to give what's important this priority? Do you want me to go to work on this for you?

At this point, there is a compelling values-based picture in front of your prospect. This picture makes the smart choice extremely obvious. There are three possible choices:

1. Yes, I want to work with you to implement this strategy.

2. Yes, I want to implement this strategy, but not with you.

3. No, I do not want to do anything.

Only one of these choices should lead to any further work on your part.

Mastery Tip

Never go to work for people who can't or won't make commitments. You will be throwing away your time and effort. Your job is to help them become aware of the truth. Their truth will usually motivate them to take action. Occasionally it will not. Ultimately, they must want to achieve their goals and fulfill their values more than you want it for them.

6. DISENGAGE FROM THE PROSPECT IF COMMITMENT IS NOT OBTAINED.

In Chapter 1, we considered in detail how and when to disengage from difficult people early in the first meeting. But you should be aware that occasionally a prospect will go through the discovery process and then refuse to make a commitment or to set another appointment.

The more you practice the values conversation, the more quickly you will be able to recognize this type of prospect, and you will disengage before you waste time in discovery with the wrong person. However, disengaging politely and firmly at this stage is just as important and empowering as doing so earlier. All you've invested is one hour. By disengaging now from someone who cannot make a commitment, you can avoid wasting 10 to 20 hours of strategy planning and follow-up time, and you can prevent an infinite amount of frustration. **Every moment you spend with a difficult person is a moment you are not investing in finding a Great Client.**

115

Build your clientele as you would build your dream home.
Poor planning and materials = poor outcome.

[Prospect.] [*Hemming and hawing, clearly is not going to commit. Even though the VBFP has specifically asked for a commitment, the prospect is avoiding making one.*]

VBFP. Obviously you're not comfortable making a commitment right now. Can you tell me what you find uncomfortable about making a commitment to take charge of your financial future?

Prospect. I really don't know. I want to think it over.

VBFP. No problem, take as much time as you need to think it over. Do whatever you need to do. This Financial Road Map represents your reality. It will not change by itself. I'm going to leave this totally in your hands. I can't go to work for you until you can make a commitment. I'll keep all the work we've done here in this file. When you decide you are ready to make a commitment, please give me a call.

If by this point the prospect can't make a commitment, it's not the VBFP's fault. Some people just can't commit. There may be something going on in their lives that is just too personal or embarrassing to tell you about. Disengage politely and don't let them take your work with them unless they paid for it. Maybe they'll call you later.

When a conversation develops like the one above, escort the noncommittal prospect to the door. Be polite, but don't go to work. You will sometimes be tempted to bargain with uncommitted prospects, imagining they will be so impressed with the strategy you create that they will immediately implement it once they see it. I recommend you don't get sucked into this time-wasting trap. Respect the quality of your work and recognize that a person's ability to make a commitment is an entirely separate matter.

7. DISCUSS SERVICES AND COST.

One beauty of Values-Based Selling is that often it isn't even necessary at this point to discuss the total cost. Reasonable people understand that a complete projection of costs before a strategy is assembled and agreed upon is ludicrous. It would be like asking an interior designer to take a good look at your house, then give a detailed estimate on redesign and furnishings. And asking a financial professional to create a complete strategy for free would be like asking that designer to complete a floorplan at no charge simply on the basis of a possibility of a commission on whatever furniture might be purchased. People in the financial services industry give away more for free than professionals in any other industry. In your role as life advisor, keep in mind the practices of business consultants: They charge you for an assessment of your business, sometimes take a commission on sales of products or services you buy, and even get paid for additional consultations as needed. All of this is based on the client's belief in the consultant's expertise— not on what the consultant is willing to give away for free.

Ken Friedman's story illustrates how people can trust you, not because they know who you are and what you do, but because they know you understand them.

Ken, a financial planner in Jacksonville, Florida, had never been to one of my workshops. However, on the recommendation of one of his mentors, he had ordered and listened to my tapes. He began using the values conversation right away. When Ken's manager hired me to do a workshop for his office, I didn't know that there was already a values-based success story in the audience. In the morning, I taught the values conversation.

During the break, Ken told me how he was getting checks for the financial plan *before* discovery. I asked him to share his experience with his peers. They were particularly interested because they had noticed the dramatic improvement in his production. Ken had written 20 financial plans in the first three months of that year, more than he had written the entire previous year. The fees for the plans plus the commissions generated upon implementation had propelled Ken to becoming one of the top producers in his company nationally.

Ken said, "I stopped bothering with the small talk, and I stopped explaining the company story, my credentials and the usefulness of financial planning. I stopped 'educating' and using statistics to scare people about the future. Instead, I set the stage and used the values conversation. I could immediately feel the difference. I couldn't believe how anxious my clients were to do whatever was necessary to create a plan that would help them fulfill their values. Price and details simply were never an issue. Whenever I asked prospects for a check before the needs analysis, they gave me one." It's not that Ken's clients would pay any amount of money for the plan. It's just that the perceived value becomes so high that only an outrageous price would seem unreasonable.

If, like Ken Friedman, you want to get a check to write a financial strategy before discovery (provided you have the proper registration and licensing to charge fees, of course), you might want to use a transition similar to his. Here's what he says after he has concluded the values conversation with a prospect.

Ken. Now that I have a clear understanding of what's important to you, the next step is simple. I can help you develop a plan to get there. First, I need to get a check from you for $500 as a deposit against the final cost of the plan. Then we do an extremely comprehensive analysis of your current financial situation and your financial goals. Just write us a check, and we'll get started right away.

When I tell this story, the response is often, "No way! People will never make a commitment to do business with a financial professional until they know exactly what they are buying and how much it will cost." Don't tell Ken that. He's working with affluent clients, earning six figures, and last year he took all of July and August off to be with his family. It's not that the clients don't care about what they're getting. They are simply more interested in getting their financial life together *now*. When they trust you and are emotionally committed to their future, they expect that you will treat them fairly and do good work. You will treat them fairly and do good work for them, won't you?

People trust you because you understand them, not because they understand you.

8. SET AN APPOINTMENT TO PRESENT THE FINANCIAL STRATEGY.

When prospects want to work with you to achieve their goals and fulfill their values, set a date and time for the next meeting. Agreeing now on the date and time accomplishes four purposes.

1. It confirms their commitment.

2. It establishes a definite deadline for you to create the plan so you can't procrastinate.

3. It avoids the awkwardness of playing telephone tag to set a second appointment.

4. It creates a sense of positive anticipation, a sense of closure and a feeling of accomplishment that they're finally taking charge of their financial future and their lives.

In the next chapter, we'll discuss the best methods to develop a financial strategy that will be quickly accepted and implemented.

Summary

- VBFPs achieve total financial discovery in the initial interview.

- These are the eight steps of the discovery process:

    1. Establish financial goals.

    2. Use the Financial Road Map.

    3. Discover all the facts about the current financial situation.

4. Chart/plot on the Financial Road Map what you've discovered.

5. Get commitment.

6. Disengage from prospects who don't, can't or won't make a commitment.

7. Discuss your services.

8. Set an appointment to present the financial strategy.

- If people trust you, they will provide full financial disclosure.

  1. People trust you because you understand them, not because they understand you.

  2. Trust does not depend on the amount of time two people have known each other; trust depends on the events that occur between them. Meaningful events build trust.

- Use values, not goals, to create buying momentum. Values are like emotional magnets that motivate people to act.

EXERCISE

Make a Financial Road Map for yourself and your family. Let yourself experience the power of "the gap" in your own financial life. Are you on track to achieve your goals and fulfill your values? Once you have a Financial Road Map of your own, you can fully appreciate how and why this visual device works so well for your prospects and clients. Notice how compelling your values are in inspiring you to do whatever

it takes to put your own financial life in order
so you can achieve your goals. After all, how
can people who are giving financial advice for a
living not be on track for financial independence
themselves? You will find yourself being much
more effective helping people with their
Financial Road Maps when you are
implementing one of your own.

NOTES

_____

_____

_____

_____

_____

_____

_____

_____

_____

_____

_____

_____

_____

_____

6. Create a Financial Strategy Masterpiece.

GEORGE

Imagine you are boarding an airplane and you happen to engage in a brief conversation with the pilot. During that conversation the pilot appears confident, focused and skilled. You trust his ability as a pilot. However, your feelings quickly change when the pilot has trouble on takeoff. As the plane falters slightly, you get an uneasy sensation of being unsafe, and you think, "Man, this pilot sounded real good, but it was all talk. There's no competence here." Trust is important. But equally important is being very good at what you do.

As a Values-Based Financial Professional (VBFP), you, too, must deliver high-quality work to reinforce and maintain the trust you have built. And you can't deliver what you've promised unless you are completely prepared. To be consistently successful, you must be good at building trust and you must be a good financial professional. In fact, I encourage you to become a brilliant financial professional.

Many financial professionals apply their work ethic to prospecting, marketing and selling instead of mastering their craft—the art of building high-trust client relationships and being a *brilliant* financial professional. Michael Jackson described the kind of dedication it takes to become brilliant when he described Fred Astaire:

> *Nobody could duplicate Mr. Astaire's ability, but what I never stop trying to emulate is his total discipline, his absolute dedication to every aspect of his art. He rehearsed, rehearsed, and rehearsed some more, until he got it just the way he wanted it. It was Fred Astaire's work ethic that few people ever discussed and even fewer could ever hope to equal.*

Presenting an accurate financial strategy provides proof that you listened. Creating a personal, accurate, effective financial strategy takes quality time. Before you begin to design such a strategy, follow these guidelines to save time and reduce stress:

- Prepare presentations only for people who trust and believe you (Great Clients).

- Never prepare a presentation without complete and accurate data.

- Prepare presentations only for people who have made a commitment to implement your recommendations when your advice meets their predetermined criteria.

Your clients' confidence in doing business with you comes from the combination of the two components of trust: the *feeling of trust* you developed with them in the first interview, and your *delivery* of what you have promised: an accurate financial strategy.

What's the point of being a brilliant financial advisor if you aren't effective at getting people to want to do business with you? And what's the point of being able to get people to want to work with you if the quality of your work isn't impressive enough to inspire people to implement your ideas and provide a consistent flow of referrals? Mastering both halves of the trust relationship is crucial to your success.

This strong bond of trust will continue to be reinforced and enhanced every time you meet with your clients. Remember, the more accurate and compelling the presentation the more rapid the implementation. Conducting a brilliant interview sets you up for success. But then you have to deliver. This is where your product knowledge, resources and experience become factors. The less product knowledge and experience you have, the more you rely on your resources (mentors, company, suppliers, strategic alliances, etc.).

To demonstrate your competence and deliver financial strategies your clients will implement right away, you will want to concentrate on four areas: *research, purpose, preparation* and *attitude*.

1. DO YOUR RESEARCH AND JUDGE BY RESULTS.

The interview was your research about the client, and the success of that interview cannot be measured by how you felt about it. Imagine Monica Seles telling the tennis line judge, "That shot couldn't have been out. It felt exactly right." World-class sports stars know that you don't gain a point or win a game on the basis of how you feel about your performance. You win based on *results*. Measurable criteria dictate how good the shot is, and the score dictates who wins the game. The same is true in financial services; the only difference is that both you and the client win. Here are some criteria of a good interview:

- **You had a compelling and emotional values conversation.** Your prospects' core values are written down in their own words.

- **You conducted a thorough goals discussion.** Using your prospects' own words, you recorded their goals:

  1. Every current goal that requires money to accomplish

  2. Every current goal that doesn't require money but can be achieved only when they are financially independent

- **You achieved total financial discovery.** Your prospects told you where all their money is, and you have copies of every important financial document.

- **You obtained commitment.** Your prospects made a commitment to meet with you again and to implement your financial advice, on the condition that it meets predetermined conditions of helping them achieve their goals and fulfill their values.

Your interview was a weak one if its only result was to discover a need to which you could sell a product.

2. STAY ON PURPOSE.

You are creating a financial strategy to achieve one purpose: to bridge the gap between where your clients are now and where they want to be so they can fulfill their values in life. Achieving their goals and fulfilling their core values is the driving benefit to the clients.

Therefore, stay focused on the clients. You work for your clients, not for a company. The company may send you the check, but the clients' decisions make that check possible. *Always* put the clients first, and you'll earn more money, get more referrals and become the clients' sole financial professional—not to mention generate the amount and quality of

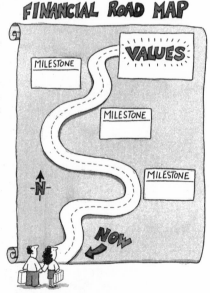

FINANCIAL RoAD MAP

The essence of the presentation is to demonstrate how your strategy, products and services help your clients bridge the gap between where they are now and where they want to be so they can enjoy the emotional payoff of fulfilling their values in life.

129

Financial Road Map®
for Living Life on Purpose

*"There are those who travel
and those who are going somewhere.
They are different, and yet
they are the same. Successful people
have this over their rivals:
they know where they are going."*
Mark Caine

**Personal Goals
"Milestones"**

Move to
bigger home
(2500 sq. ft.

Where are you today?

Cash Reserves		Growth	
Now	**To Be**	**Now**	**To Be**
$14,000	$28,000	(Fill in with current amounts)	(Fill in with target amounts)
2 mo. living expenses	4 mo. living expenses		
Action: $500/month for 28 months		**Action:** Max out Qual. $ $ Into Equity Vehicles $ Into Fixed Vehicles	
Debt		**Risk Management**	
Now	**To Be**	**Now**	**To Be**
$9,000 unsecured	$0 unsecured	Disability Health Liability Life Funded Buy/sell 2nd to die	Protected to finance events that could reduce or eliminate cash reserves, growth funds, or incur debt
$200,000 mortgage	Pay on current mortgage schedule		
Action: $1,000/month for 9 months		**Action:** Insurance review and increase as necessary	

130

"What's Important to You?"

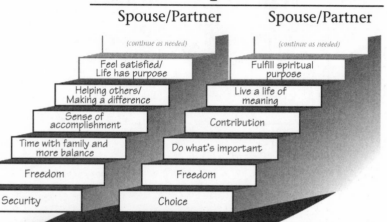

Spouse/Partner   Spouse/Partner

(continue as needed)   *(continue as needed)*

Feel satisfied/ Life has purpose	Fulfill spiritual purpose
Helping others/ Making a difference	Live a life of meaning
Sense of accomplishment	Contribution
Time with family and more balance	Do what's important
Freedom	Freedom
Security	Choice

Personal Goals "Milestones"
Retire by age 62

Personal Goals "Milestones"
Send kids to college 1. Scott (in 10 yrs.) 2. Kelly (in 12 yrs.)

"The Financial Road Map has helped me become totally comfortable asking for and getting fees for financial planning. It keeps my clients focused on what's important, motivates them to tell me where all their assets are in the first meeting, helps them make commitments to follow my advice right away, and re-establishes their determination to implement my recommendations every time we have a follow-up session. The results have been thousands of dollars in revenue and a lot more commissions per client. This is the single best tool I've ever used for helping my clients take charge of their financial lives. Thank you!"

JOSEPH SPENCER
The Spencer Group

To receive a free sample of a blank Financial Road Map by mail, fax your address and request to Bachrach & Associates, Inc. at (858) 558-0748, or e-mail us at info@bachrachvbs.com. *This printed document cannot be faxed or e-mailed to you.*

"Where are you today?"

Cash Reserves		Growth Strategy	
Where are you now?	**Where do you want to be?**	**Where are you now?**	**Where do you want to be?**
		Action: _____ **Objective:** • Achieve goals/milestones *Benefit/Why do it?* ★ It feels good! This is the money that achieves your goals! Lifetime strategy of 8–12% average annual return over time	
Action: _____ **Objective:** • Prepared for emergency • Save for big purchases *in advance* *Benefit/Why do it?* ★ It feels good! Once built, the deposit goes toward growth.			
Debt		**Risk Management Insurance**	
Where are you now?	**Where do you want to be?**	**Where are you now?**	**Where do you want to be?**
		Action: _____ **Objective:** • Mitigate impact and reduce risk of unpleasant events • Block negative consequences of events that could prevent financial strategy from unfolding and creating the life we want *Benefit/Why do it?* ★ It feels good! ★ It's prudent.	
Action: _____ **Objective:** • Debt reduction/elimination • Eliminate enemy of growth • No upstream swimming *Benefit/Why do it?* ★ It feels good! Once reduced or eliminated, the payment goes toward growth.			

"Imagine what life will be like when . . . "
- you have a prudent amount of cash reserves
- your debt is gone
- your risks are completely mitigated
- your growth strategy is flourishing/moving you toward your goals

"Give me some words . . ."
"Imagine how you would feel . . . "

---

business that will make any company happy with your performance.

Show your clients how each quadrant of their Current Financial Situation will be steadily improving as they follow their financial strategy. Their debt will be moving toward zero, their cash reserves will be growing, their risk management will be strong, and their growth strategy will move them toward their goals.

This new reality can be accomplished through their relationship with you: You help to create the strategy then help to implement it.

3. PREPARE, PREPARE AND PREPARE SOME MORE.

The perfect preparation is overpreparation. For example, I've given hundreds of keynote speeches and workshops in the financial industry. Still, I always use extensive preprogram questionnaires, including requests for marketing material, discovery interview tools, sales training materials and corporate annual reports. We interview the producers and leaders of each company or group to whom I am speaking. I overprepare so I can be confident that I know my client and won't make a foolish mistake on the platform.

In a way, you take the platform every time you present your professional opinion on how clients should invest their assets or insure themselves. The more you prepare, the more confident you will be during your presentation. If you have confidence in yourself, your clients will have confidence in you, too.

> **Part of generating trust is being extremely competent.**
>
> **Part of being extremely competent is being overprepared.**

For your presentation, it's much better to have lots of backup documentation and never use it than to lack the backup documentation if you need it. By the same token, you do not have to say everything you planned to say or use every chart you are prepared to use. Professional sports teams prepare for many scenarios they hope never to use. The players on a football team are always ready to use the two-minute drill, but they hope they will never need to use it. Golfers practice hitting out of sand, but they hope never to need to use this skill.

My skydiving jump master spent hours teaching me skills I hoped never to use, including what to do if my parachute didn't open. Was I disappointed because my parachute did open and I didn't have to use everything I was prepared for? Of course not—I was thankful to know what to do, and even more thankful not to have to do it.

To prepare an accurate financial strategy, you must know all the details. If you find that important data is missing, call your client immediately to ask about it. Otherwise, your strategy will be less than accurate and your presentation will be less than compelling.

"The will to succeed is important, but what's more important is to prepare."

BOBBY KNIGHT

A Logical Approach to Preparing a Financial Strategy

Although you want to appeal to your clients' emotional reasons to implement their financial strategy, the preparation of that strategy follows a logical process:

1. Review your meeting notes.

2. Listen to an audiotape of the interview with the client. (I'll teach you how to tape every interview in Chapter 12.)

3. Crunch the numbers (using software provided by your company or commercially available, such as Financial Profiles™).*

4. Call your clients immediately if you are missing any information necessary to create the best plan for them.

5. Use your resources (e.g., case preparation experts, managers, mentors, books, tapes, product specialists).

6. Select appropriate products.

7. Prepare the presentation—verbal and visual, conceptual and detailed.

8. Prepare all paperwork needed for every idea so clients can easily execute each component of the plan.

9. Practice! Practice by videotaping, audiotaping or role-playing with friends and colleagues. Be so comfortable with what you are going to say that you don't have to think about it. This frees your thoughts to be totally in tune with your client. Be overprepared!

You can order from Financial Profiles by calling (800) 237-6335.

As you prepare each recommendation within the strategy, answer for yourself the following questions. Clarify these completely so you can explain the risks of implementing the strategy and the risks of not implementing the strategy.

- What happens when my client implements these recommendations?
- What will happen in five years as a result of implementation?
- What will happen over my client's lifetime as a result of implementation?
- What will happen immediately, in five years and over the clients' lifetime if they do not implement these recommendations?

Preparing honest answers to these questions will help you manage the clients' expectations. Client expectations that are too high set you up for failure. Client expectations that are too low may not be compelling enough for the client to take action now. Be sure you can deliver what you promise.

One final note on preparation: Be sure to use all the appropriate financial products and services.

It disturbs me to see some financial professionals giving their clients less than the best advice because they are familiar with only part of the product spectrum. Wirehouse-trained financial professionals sometimes rely too heavily on securities products and underutilize annuities and life insurance. Some of their clients who have long time horizons are paying tax on mutual fund gains and dividends, when that money could be accumulating tax-deferred or tax-free. I know you don't need a lesson on tax-free compounding versus taxable compounding, so I'll stop there; you get the idea.

Equally disturbing are insurance agents who use insurance products to meet all financial objectives, selling their clients annuities in qualified retirement accounts when mutual funds would accomplish the same result with lower fees. I have heard some valid explanations for selling annuities and variable life inside qualified retirement accounts. I suspect the more common reason in many cases, however, is YTS (yield to salesperson) because annuities and variable life don't have commission breakpoints like mutual funds. Or because it's all the agent knows. Or because securities commissions don't count toward validating a contract or qualifying for the President's Club. Or because the company simply doesn't train its producers in the full product spectrum.

Some wirehouse financial consultants seem to feel that selling insurance products is somehow beneath them. Therefore, many stockbrokers leave huge amounts of money on the table and underserve their clients in the areas of risk management, estate planning and charitable giving. Bank investment representatives carry similar biases depending on where they were trained and on product availability. These tendencies are so prevalent that you might consider checking the full spectrum of products you are offering to determine if an adjustment is in order. Your clients deserve recommendations that are best for them, so I highly recommend being familiar with all products if you are not already.

The Presentation Planning Worksheet

Preparation equals confidence. For each of your clients' financial goals, prepare a worksheet before the meeting so that you know the answers to the most likely questions they will ask about your recommendations.

You may want to develop your own list of questions to help you best communicate with your clients. The questions I recommend are listed below. Remember, you will want to know the answers to all the questions, even if you don't use them all in your presentation.

CLIENT'S NAME:

GOAL/PERSONAL MILESTONE:

1. Which product(s) will best help my client achieve this financial goal?

_____

_____

_____

_____

2. Which values are specifically related to the achievement of this goal?

_____

_____

_____

_____

3. Of the many benefits this product or service will deliver, what are the three primary benefits to this client?

_____

_____

_____

4. Which features of this product or service generate these benefits?

_____

_____

_____

_____

5. How will the benefits help the client more effectively achieve this goal and fulfill his or her values?

_____

_____

_____

_____

6. What are the consequences of not implementing the financial strategy?

_____

_____

_____

_____

7. What emotional payoff will my client enjoy as a result of utilizing this specific product, idea or service?

_____

_____

_____

_____

8. What will I say to stimulate this emotional response? (Be sure the client feels the emotional pull.)

_____

_____

_____

_____

_____

9. What brochures, aids or evidence do I need to support or prove my recommendations? (You won't necessarily show the client all of this, but you want to be prepared to use it as backup information.)

_____

_____

_____

_____

In addition to the nine goal-specific questions listed above, think about the following five general questions in order to help your clients make the smartest decisions.

1. Can my new clients really achieve their financial goals, given their current situation and time frame?
❑ Yes ❑ No

2. Will my recommendations/strategy ultimately put them in a position to achieve their goals, become financially independent and fulfill their values?
❑ Yes ❑ No

3. Can they afford to implement this financial strategy?
❑ Yes ❑ No

4. In what order of priority should they implement the strategy if they cannot afford to implement everything right away?

A _____

B _____

C _____

5. Am I promising more than I can deliver? Will my clients be expecting the impossible? Could I be setting myself up for failure (or a lawsuit)?
❏ Yes ❏ No

If this seems too time-consuming to you, consider the time wasted preparing and making presentations that never get seen or implemented. Consider the time and money wasted on prospecting and marketing because many financial professionals don't have clients who are impressed enough to provide a steady flow of referrals.

4. HAVE AN ATTITUDE.

My friend Tom Olivo is a great fly fisherman. Tom catches twice as many fish as I do. Some of it has to do with his skill. A lot of it has to do with his attitude. Tom says, "I expect to catch a fish on every cast." Do the fish know this and hopelessly give themselves up to him? Sometimes it seems that they do. He's certainly a very skilled angler, but I believe his attitude and expectations do make a difference.

Don Shula said, "I expect to win every game." Of course, Don didn't win every game. However, he won more games than any coach in the history of the National Football League, and he is the only NFL coach in history with an undefeated season. One reason he won is that he expected to win. He expected to win because he won. What a wonderful loop to be stuck in!

Think positively, be confident and expect your clients to take action. Adopt the characteristics of the VBFP:

- **Expect the clients to buy.**
- **Expect the clients to take action.**
- **Expect the clients to implement your ideas.**
- **Expect the clients to follow through on their commitments.**
- **Expect to get referrals.**

Preparation makes it easy for clients to say yes. Your confident attitude makes it difficult for clients to say no.

Confidence and positive expectations complement each other. If you have confidence in your ability, confidence in the financial strategizing process and confidence in the products you're selling, you naturally expect the client to take action on your advice. When clients fulfill your positive expectations and implement your ideas, your confidence is in turn reinforced.

Serve as your clients' guide to help them create the life they want. As you look at their goals and values and consider the options, always do what is best for them. Remember, you're a life advisor who specializes in money.

Now that you've mastered the art of strategy preparation, let's move on to presentation.

Summary

The financial strategy you prepare is proof  you listened to the client. As you begin your preparation, keep the following four guidelines in mind:

1. Do your research and judge by results, not by feelings. Good skills during the interview result in obtaining the information you need to plan the client's specific strategy. Here are the criteria for a good interview:

   - A compelling and emotional values conversation

   - A thorough goals discussion

   - Total financial discovery

   - Commitment from your clients

   - Staying on purpose

2. Prepare, prepare, prepare—so you will have the extreme confidence that indicates extreme competence to your clients. It's always better to have more documentation and details than you will need than not to have the one piece of documentation or detail you do need. Be knowledgeable about the full spectrum of financial resources available, so you can tailor your recommendations to your clients' particular circumstances.

3. Approach the preparation of a financial strategy logically, using a Presentation Planning Worksheet.

4. Expect success. Expect the clients to take action.

EXERCISE

i Take out the file of a client who was a one-sale-only customer. Look at your notes for presenting a strategy to this client. See if you can prepare a Presentation Planning Worksheet, answering the worksheet questions to develop your strategy. If you find you are lacking pieces of information, call the client and go through the values conversation on the phone. Then ask the client to come in for some additional information about creating a financial strategy.

Use what you have learned in this chapter to prepare a complete financial strategy that will turn this one-sale customer into a lifetime high-trust client who depends on you for all financial services.

NOTES

_____

_____

_____

_____

_____

_____

_____

_____

7. Unveil Your Masterpiece With Impact!

The financial strategy you have prepared becomes tangible evidence that affirms the trust you generated in the first meeting. As you begin the presentation, you are starting to develop the second component of trust: delivering what you promised.

- Your strategy must deliver on your promises.
- Your strategy must provide evidence you listened to the client.

Trust is especially reinforced when you help your clients in areas where they know you don't earn a commission. Keep in mind that the premise of your presentation is helping your clients bridge the gap between where they are now and where they want to be, to fulfill their values in life.

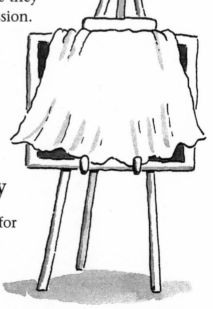

Introducing the Strategy

When you see your clients for the second scheduled meeting, keep the social amenities brief. This is a business meeting; respect your clients' time; be friendly, not verbose. What your clients really want to talk about is the strategy you've been working on to help them achieve their goals and fulfill their values. Like a travel agent helping a customer plan a trip around the world, the Values-Based Financial Professional (VBFP) has an important task to accomplish. You need to stay focused on explaining your strategy for your clients' financial journey.

Recap your clients' values, financial goals and current financial situation. Effective visual representation of the gap between their current financial situation and their personal milestones—and ultimately fulfilling their values—elicits an emotional response, which is the most powerful way to begin your second meeting. Use their Financial Road Map to graphically represent your clients' financial portrait.

VBFP. *[Restating the clients' values and pointing to the Financial Road Map.]* In our first meeting, you told me that it is important for you to make smart choices about your money so you can ———.

[Naming the goals and pointing to the Financial Road Map.] You also shared with me that you have some specific financial goals.

I have carefully reviewed your current financial position based on your financial documents. As you can see, there is a gap between where you are now and where you want to be. My job is to help you bridge that gap so you not only can achieve these goals but ultimately can also enjoy the feeling of fulfilling those values that are important to you. I have come up with a strategy designed specifically to do that for you. Are you ready to review it?

I have deliberately chosen not to provide specific language for explaining particular products because this is already your expertise, but I do want to emphasize these two general guidelines.

1. Other than legally required disclosures, less is better.

2. Financial common sense dictates that the following areas be taken care of by the person who is on the path of financial success.

   - Risk management: appropriate liability, health, disability, long-term care and life insurance
   - Debt elimination
   - Cash reserves
   - Investments and strategies for paying for future events like college, retirement or financial independence
   - Estate preservation, business continuation and charitable giving when appropriate
   - Current income: allocated assets for preservation, growth and income for already retired clients

You may not choose to sell all these products, but it is still incumbent upon you to be sure all these bases are covered if you intend to be your clients' primary financial resource and trusted advisor. VBFPs care about the whole client, not just the parts that generate commissions.

Focus on Emotions

People buy on emotion. Even analytical people, such as engineers, buy on emotion. Think about each product or service in terms of the emotion first, the benefit that created this emotion second and the product feature that triggered this benefit third. Present your recommendations in just this order: emotion, benefit, feature. Here's an example to demonstrate such a presentation.

> **VBFP.** In our first meeting you told me you want to be financially independent by the time you are 62 [*goal/personal milestone*] so you can have a sense of freedom and accomplishment that helps you fulfill your ultimate purpose in life [*values = emotion*]. With that in mind, I have selected an investment that will give you the benefit of long-term growth, which the stock market provides [*benefit*], while being diversified enough to keep the risk manageable [*benefit*]. This investment is a professionally managed portfolio that is distrib-

uted among three asset classes [*features*]. Based on your situation, I believe investing $50,000 of your liquid cash will be a crucial part of your strategy. Are there any details you need to know in order to be as confident as I am that this is a sound move for you?

Express yourself with confidence and give them only the details they need to implement the recommended strategy. The more your new clients trust you, the less detail they need before they act on your advice.

During the presentation, stay focused.

- Focus on emotional rather than logical reasons to motivate action.

- Focus on major issues rather than minor details.

- Focus on the most important issue:

VBFP. You came to me because you wanted a financial strategy. We put together a financial strategy. Now the key is to implement it. If you implement the strategy, you can get tremendous value from our time. If you don't implement the strategy, you will get zero value from our time.

The truth has power. Use it!

Closing With Values

I have a three-question strategy that will help you either obtain a commitment to implement or weed out the procrastinators who plague the lives of many financial professionals. Ask the questions and follow the directions below.

QUESTION #1

> **VBFP.** You asked me to develop a strategy for you that would help you get from where you are now financially to the point of being able to accomplish these results:
>
> - Minimize your financial risks
>
> - Achieve your goals [*Restate the clients' goals: send the children to college, provide enough capital base to generate the desired retirement income, etc.*]
>
> - Get what's important to you [*Restate the clients' core values in their own words.*]
>
> Is that right?

If the answer is yes, move on to question 2; if the answer is no, clarify and obtain a yes answer before moving on to question 2. If you cannot obtain a yes, then the clients don't think you understand their goals or what's important. Either you really blew it along the way, or someone who should have been screened out earlier slipped by.

QUESTION #2

> **VBFP.** [*Pointing to the clients' goals and values on the Financial Road Map.*] Is it clear how the strategy I have developed for you will protect you against the inherent financial risks of life, while also providing the dollars to bridge the gap between where you are now and where you want to be?

If the answer is yes, move on to question 3; if the answer is no, clarify and receive a yes answer before moving on to question 3. Although it's unlikely you will get this far and be unable to get agreement, if you cannot obtain a yes, you need to have a discussion about their hesitance to move forward. And you may have to disengage.

QUESTION #3

> **VBFP.** If you were ever going to implement a strategy that would [*accomplish the clients' goals and fulfill their values*], when would be the best time to get started?

You're looking for an answer like "now," "soon," "right away" or "yesterday." If you receive any other answer, you need to reestablish with your clients the importance of implementing their financial strategy to achieve their goals and fulfill their values. If you cannot do that, you have no real choice but to politely disengage.

Creating a financial strategy that is not implemented is a waste of time for everybody involved.

Some financial professionals have such a high degree of confidence in their strategies that they ask clients to sign a legal disclaimer if the clients don't want to implement some part of the recommended game plan. The dialogue sounds like this:

VBFP. You can do whatever you want with your money. Ultimately, it's your choice. But I need you to sign this disclaimer. It basically says that I told you what I think is the best course of action and that you are choosing not to follow my advice. I just need you to sign this so that legally, if it ever comes up, my advice was clear, but you decided to go another way.

More often than not, the client will respond with the following:

Client. Do you really feel that strongly about this recommendation?

VBFP. Yes, I really do feel that strongly about it.

Client. I guess we'll go with it, then.

If you don't feel that strongly when you make a recommendation, perhaps you shouldn't be making it. That's one way to know for yourself whether or not your reommendations are appropriate. This is not a manipulative, strong-arm tactic designed to back your clients into a corner. The competent financial professional makes appropriate recommendations and expects people to take action. People have the right to waste their own time. You have the right to not let them waste yours.

Executing the Paperwork

Finally, have all the necessary paperwork organized and ready to go so your new clients can implement their strategy immediately. Expect them to buy! It's good for them. And it's good for you.

Actions speak louder than words. People want to receive financial advice from a professional who is organized and has the details covered.

Financial Strategies for Clients Who Cannot Implement Immediately

What if your new clients cannot afford to implement an entire strategy immediately? In such a case, you need to take the following steps:

- Help them implement the parts they can afford today.
- Get their commitment to implement the rest of the strategy over time.
- Be a coach and hold them accountable to execute the strategy.

Make sure you keep priorities in the correct order. Some clients may want to start investing for college funds and avoid or delay paying for disability insurance. That's the wrong order. They'll never save enough for college for their children if they lose their income because of disability. It also doesn't make sense to make investments for a 10% gain when you have 14% interest-charging balances on credit cards (and the interest isn't even tax-deductible). Stick to your professional guns. You may occasionally lose a sale, but you'll gain more good, profitable clients by acting responsibly, ethically and intelligently. Salespeople sell what people want to buy. Trusted advisors counsel people to make the best long-term decisions. So what's wrong with just selling people what they want to buy? First, it takes no skill; second, in the financial services business, selling people what they want to buy can get you in trouble.

For those people who must face changing their habits to fulfill their values, the presentation meeting can seem like a brisk encounter with reality. What it takes to live a financially successful life will start settling in for your new clients as you talk to them. The point is not to make the process painless; the point is to make it happen—to start your clients along the path that will help them fulfill their core values.

If cash flow is a problem for your new clients, they have three options: 1) earn more money, 2) change their current spending habits or 3) fail to achieve their financial goals. I'm not saying you should judge the clients good or bad for whatever choice they make, but if they decide their financial goals aren't worth the necessary work, they will not be good clients for you. They have to want their own success more than you do. This is rubber-meets-the-road time. If they will not implement, then you must walk away.

For those who want to achieve their financial goals but have little control over their income, the only logical approach may be a change in spending habits. You can use a cash-flow analysis to determine where adjustments can be made. The analysis is simple. Just determine these two things:

1. How much is coming in?
2. Where is it going?

There are many effective ways to help your clients get their finances together in the areas in which you don't personally want to work. Go to the bookstore and compile a list of books and tapes that teach people how to manage a budget and get out of debt. Have your assistant maintain a list of low-interest credit cards your clients can transfer their balances to while they pay them off. Debt-management software is available for those who want to create a pay-off schedule. Be a value-added resource, not just a commissioned financial products salesperson.

An Ethical Dilemma

What do you do when your clients' risk tolerance isn't high enough to achieve the goals they say they want to achieve? Do you sell them what they are comfortable with and guarantee a financial shortfall but no loss of principal? Or do you recommend something with more risk that will probably achieve their goals but isn't guaranteed?

With today's legal and compliance environment, you might feel safe selling the low-risk vehicle. But today's legal climate may not prevail in the future when your clients realize they haven't gotten where they wanted to go. Can you imagine being sued by clients—and losing—for not telling them, because of their risk tolerance, about products they needed to achieve their goals? This is like a doctor who recommends a sedentary lifestyle to clients who are overweight and have high blood pressure—simply because they have low exercise tolerance.

I foresee a time in the future when clients successfully sue their advisors and agents for this kind of financial malpractice, for selling products that were guaranteed not to reach the goal the clients wanted to achieve. There might be a day when you or a colleague will be appearing before an arbitration panel and will lose, not because the client lost money, but because recommendations were not made for potential returns high enough to achieve the clients' goals.

Conventional wisdom would say, Don't sell them anything that isn't within their risk tolerance. As a VBFP, however, you must help your clients recognize this catch-22. After all, you didn't help them create a Financial Road Map only to ignore the ultimate destination.

The VBFP chooses to work only with clients who are realistic. Remember, risk tolerance isn't like an allergy; it's completely under the clients' control. **Clients can change their preferences when faced with the choice of either taking a little more risk or not achieving their goals.** What's more, if you and your clients create an accurate financial strategy and then the client is not willing to do what it takes to make it a reality, then you must walk away. On a positive note, the VBFP will usually have developed such a high-trust relationship that he or she will never have to do this.

Be a Professional.

Imagine yourself going to Dr. Bonehead's office. After the doctor has checked your test results and established the goals for treatment, he says, "Here is a prescription that, when taken as directed, should relieve your pain. But you should know that this medication is manufactured by three different companies. Therefore, I have copied the research data submitted by each of these companies for FDA approval. Read this information carefully, call the FDA and then tell the pharmacist which manufacturer you prefer."

Only a bonehead would make a prescription and then ask you to do all the research to choose a brand.

Wouldn't you think it strange that Dr. Bonehead is asking you to make a medical decision a doctor really should be making? If you trusted this doctor, wouldn't you take his advice without too much, if any, detailed questioning?

Your clients want your advice, too. Remember, your clients want someone they can trust, who is knowledgeable and competent, to tell them what to do.

Your clients expect you to know more about financial details than they do. If they trust your advice, they will quickly agree to implement your strategy. After all, they want to achieve their goals and fulfill their values even more than you want to earn fees or commissions.

Do Not Overeducate.

Some financial professionals get so excited about what they know that they want to share all the details with their clients. That's a normal temptation, but it needs to be suppressed. **The objective of presenting the financial strategy is not to prove how smart you are; it's to help your clients get on the right financial path.** Your game plan should be designed for quick, reasonable implementation by the prospect who then becomes your client for life. Stick to that game plan.

Do not overeducate. Your clients need to understand just enough to implement, because implementation is what will help them achieve their goals and fulfill their values. Of course, there are legal disclosure requirements that must be met. Make sure you meet those requirements without overkill.

Now that you've earned it, the next chapter is about maintaining a lifetime of client trust.

Summary

The following guidelines will help you powerfully present your recommended financial strategy:

- Focus on emotions. Remember the order: emotion, benefit, feature. First evoke the client's emotions by reviewing values and then discuss the benefits of the recommended action, and only then explain the features of the strategy you are selling. Use the Financial Road Map.

- Be professional. Do not overeducate. The goal of your presentation is to help your clients get on the right financial path, not to show them how smart you are.

- Close with values. A three-question process that starts with the clients' values and ends with commitment will quickly cement a relationship with good clients and will help eliminate the difficult clients from your life.

- Execute the paperwork. Your new clients are ready to buy. Make it easy for them!

- If new clients cannot implement the recommended strategy immediately, take these two steps:
  1. Help them implement what they can afford today.
  2. Get their commitment to implement the rest of the strategy over time,

even if it means they must choose
to earn more money or change their
current spending habits in order to
achieve their financial goals.

- Be a coach and hold them accountable
to execute the strategy. If the clients' risk
tolerance is not high enough to accept the
risks needed to achieve their goals and
fulfill their values, clarify the situation
for them. They have the choice of either
lowering their goals or increasing their
risk tolerance to the level necessary. If
they cannot do either, just walk away—
you cannot help them fulfill their values.

EXERCISE 1

Take your notes from one of the values
conversations you conducted in Chapter 2.
From those notes, create an opening statement
for a financial presentation like the one at the
beginning of this chapter. Address emotion,
benefit and features in that order. Just for
practice, this can be a fictional statement, but
a real statement based on your preparation
is even better. In any case, use it to practice
focusing on emotions and to break the old habit
of the "features and benefits" presentation. If
this feels awkward, try it again. Practice until
it feels comfortable.

EXERCISE 2

Take a close look at a real presentation you are preparing now.

- Does it follow the guidelines listed in the summary above?

- Are you prepared to discuss the options if the client cannot implement everything immediately?

- Are you so convinced that this is an accurate, appropriate recommendation that you would ask the clients to sign a legal disclaimer if they weren't willing to follow your advice?

NOTES

_____

_____

_____

_____

_____

_____

_____

_____

_____

_____

_____

PART III

Getting It Was One Thing.

Keeping It Is Everything.

8. Maintain Trust by Adding Value.

Earning and maintaining trust must be approached deliberately. Many people today either promise and don't deliver or promise what they simply can't deliver. As your potential clients are exposed to more people who don't deliver, they tend to trust everybody they meet a little less. So it's important that you continue to provide evidence you're trustworthy and to show you care about your clients. Remember: Your clients are someone else's prospects.

Adding Value to the Client Relationship

One of the most common client complaints is how little contact there is "after the sale." The trend toward fee-based financial services is a clear indicator that many clients are willing to pay for regular contact with their advisors. They feel they are receiving more value, so it makes sense that they pay more money.

The philosophy of Values-Based Selling is thinking of yourself as more than a financial professional. You help people with their entire lives. Your expertise is about money and financial choices, but the impact of good financial health goes far beyond the financial arena.

One of my favorite things is to teach financial professionals that giving people financial advice is not about money. The diagram on page 169 illustrates that financial health is a key piece in the puzzle of our lives, primarily because it interlocks with every other aspect.

Smart Financial Choices
Impact the Quality of Your Life.

Perhaps you got into this business because you couldn't get a "real" job or you heard that stockbrokers make a lot of money, or someone said you'd be good in sales. Or maybe you got recruited by an insurance or financial planning company who promised you unlimited income and control of your own life. Whatever your reason, it's critical that you understand the power you have to influence people's lives. By helping others achieve their goals and fulfill their values, you help them lead successful lives.

There are five basic pieces to a successful life: mental health, physical health, relationship health, spiritual health and financial health. All aspects of your "health" are connected like a puzzle. There is a relationship between helping people lead financially healthy lives and the impact on their mental health, physical health, relationship health and spiritual health.

Perhaps the most obvious connection is the way sound financial health reduces stress and brightens a person's mental outlook. What about the relationship between financial health and physical health? Because stress is related to illness, lowering financial stress can impact physical health. Have you ever sacrificed a workout because you needed to do more business? I have. If you were financially independent, would you be in a better position to pursue some of your fitness goals? Probably. The relationship between financial health and physical health becomes obvious. Similarly, there is clearly a relationship between financial health and relationship health. Money problems can shatter a marriage, even among the wealthy. Financial health can have a positive impact on relationships with family, friends and business associates.

What about spiritual health? Surely it is true that people can be flat broke and be very spiritual. However, isn't it also true that most religious organizations seek financial success so they can spread their beliefs and do good works for others? Of course. If nothing else, financial challenges can be a distraction from our spiritual focus. Although it doesn't have to be this way, many people do pursue the fulfillment of more spiritual values once they have attained financial success.

The bottom line is that we live in a society with certain financial expectations. Having our financial lives together gives us the time to be more involved in the things that are actually more important.

So, in addition to coaching people to solid financial health, you help them have a better overall quality of life. Your work helps them have better relationship health, better mental health, better physical health and even better spiritual health. The net benefit of your work is not really about money at all. When you help people take charge of their financial lives, you are doing a lot more good than might be immediately apparent. The value-added ideas in this chapter support this premise and your role as a life advisor specializing in money.

Customer service experts agree it is far less expensive to maintain an existing client than it is to find a new one. Moreover, satisfied clients continue to bring in referrals, so, in effect, your clients will do all your prospecting and marketing for you! (We will address this more in Chapter 9.)

With that in mind, every informational tool you create or use should be an investment in the relationship. Most financial newsletters, for example, do not demonstrate caring; they just deliver financial facts. We all know the saying that people do not care how much you know until they know how much you care. But you can't just say to someone, "I care." Caring is best demonstrated through actions not words.

Using the value-added pieces presented in this chapter will show your clients you are a person who cares about their entire quality of life. It is important that your clients feel you care about them as people and not just piles of money from which you earn commissions.

The Value-Added Pieces

To continue building a trust-based relationship "after the sale," you can mail clients ideas that positively impact their lives. These value-added ideas contribute to some aspect of clients' health: mental, physical, relationship, spiritual or financial. Their purpose is to make deposits into the "emotional bank account," not to set them up for another sale. This is a concept introduced by Stephen R. Covey in his book *The 7 Habits of Highly Effective People.*

I suggest single-sheet mailing pieces that you send once a month. This regular contact will show your clients that you care about them even when you're not working on a specific financial issue. Each value-added piece is either accompanied by a cover letter on your letterhead or has a preprinted note attached (see the following sample).

NOTE WITH VALUE-ADDED PIECE

Dear [*Client's/Prospect's Name*]:
Enclosed is an idea that may be useful
to you. I hope you find it valuable.

Sincerely,
[*VBFP's Name*]

Creating the Value-Added System

Adopting a value-added strategy can be accomplished easily and efficiently if you approach the task systematically.

1. Create the value-added pieces.

2. Implement a consistent mailing strategy.

Begin by finding 12 brief pieces for each calendar year, to be mailed monthly. It takes less than one or two days to identify all you'll need for the entire year. Look through several issues of a newspaper for articles that are not time sensitive. Call or write the newspaper to ask for permission, and be sure to use the correct credit line to give credit to both the author and the source.

Ask the author or publisher (whoever owns the copyright) to send or fax you a letter granting permission. Even better, send or fax to the author or publisher a specific request in standard release language that can be signed and sent back. Remember always to use the article exactly as it appeared in the original source and to affix an appropriate credit line.

Here is a standard form I use to request permission. (Obviously, I'm not a copyright attorney, so you should have your own lawyer review whatever documentation you decide to use.)

PERMISSION REQUEST LETTER

Permissions Department
[Publisher]
[Publisher's Address]

The purpose of this letter is to secure permission to reprint the attached selection from *[Name of Work]*. I will distribute reprints to my clients, free of charge. I will, of course, give credit in whatever form you prefer.

If the copyright to the selection is no longer held by you and has reverted to another party, a reference address would be greatly appreciated. For your convenience, I've included a release on the bottom of this letter.

Please advise if any further permission is required.

If you need any additional information, please feel free to contact me at *[phone number]*. Thank you in advance for your assistance.

Regards,

[VBFP's Name]

Name _____ Title _____

Company _____

Address _____

Phone Number _____

Signature, Title _____ Date _____

You can also search computer files for public-domain articles. The Internet and on-line services also have lots of material available.

Following are samples of value-added pieces we created for one of our clients. Notice the general interest of the topic: "10 Rules for Being Human." This could fall into the category of spiritual health.

Allmerica

ALLMERICA
FINANCIAL

Place your photo here if desired

Because smart financial choices impact your quality of life.

Ten Rules for Being Human

1. You will receive a body. You may like it or hate it, but it's yours to keep for the entire period.

2. You will learn lessons. You are enrolled in a full-time informal school called "life."

3. There are no mistakes, only lessons. Growth is a process of trial, error, and experimentation. The "failed" experiments are as much a part of the process as the experiments that ultimately "work."

4. Lessons are repeated until they are learned. A lesson will be presented to you in various forms until you have learned it. When you have earned it, you can go on to the next lesson.

5. Learning lessons does not end. There's no part of life that doesn't contain lessons. If you're alive, that means there are still lessons to be learned.

6. "There" is no better than "here." When your "there" has become a "here," you will simply obtain another "there" that will look better than "here."

7. Other people are merely mirrors of you. You cannot love or hate something about another person unless it reflects something you love or hate about yourself.

8. What you make of your life is up to you. You have all the tools and resources you need. What you do with them is up to you. The choice is yours.

9. Your answers lie within you. The answers to life's questions lie within you. All you need to do is look, listen, and trust.

10. You will forget all this.

Anonymous

To get more mileage from your mailings, you can design your own unique header and slogan so that your clients and referrals will immediately recognize the pieces as they open them. The one in this example was created by a graphic artist for one of my clients.

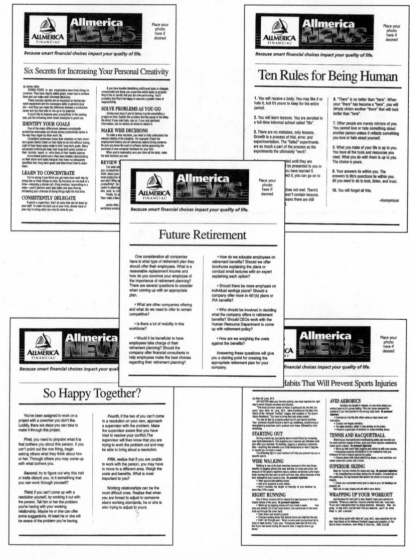

Value-added pieces contribute to clients' health in several areas: financial (center); mental, spiritual, physical, relationship (clockwise from top left).

Mail the Value-Added Pieces Systematically.

Start mailing the value-added pieces right away to your existing clients. But this is a system, so automate it before you begin. Let's say, for example, that you are reading this book in May and want to start a system this month.

All you need is a large box or shelves with one separator for each month. Behind each separator, place addressed, stamped envelopes for each existing client with the value-added piece for that month. Postdate everything. At the beginning of June, mail out all the value-added pieces for that month, and do the same at the start of each month for the remainder of the year.

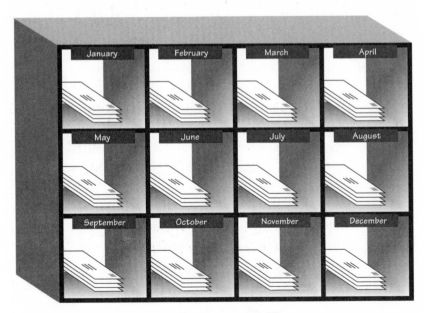

The Future Mailbox

May 15, 2001

Since writing this chapter in 1996 we received many, many requests for a simpler, turn-key system. The result is the monthly *Values-Based Financial Planning (VBFP) Newsletter.* For a more detailed description of the *VBFP Newsletter* see the promotional information in the back of the book.

In December of this year, identify and obtain permisison to reprint the 12 value-added pieces you want to use next year. Reproduce each piece and address, stamp and file the envelopes for that year (one per month per client). This is a good activity for you or an assistant during the normally slow time between December 15 and January 1.

Whenever you get new clients, put them into the system right away. If two of your prospects become clients in August, for example, they should receive the monthly mailings for September through December of that year. They then become part of the regular monthly mailings and receive all 12 pieces during each following year.

The New Client Relationship Gift

After the second meeting and once your clients have implemented their strategy, you may want to send a small gift. It serves as a tangible, positive reminder to continue to implement their strategy and to call you with their questions. It can also evoke positive emotions about their new relationship with you.

One gift I have used successfully is a crystal clock that costs $25. If this sounds like a good idea, remember these guidelines.

- Place a sticker on the bottom of the clock with your name and phone number.

- Resist the temptation to plaster your logo on the front. Nobody wants to decorate a home or office with your company's logo. The clock serves as a reminder of the quality of your relationship without overselling. (You remember who gave you the gifts in your home or office, don't you?)

- Send a brief note.

NOTE WITH GIFT

> *Dear* [*Client's/Prospect's Name*]:
> *Every time you look at this clock, you will be reminded that it is a good time to be in charge of your financial life. I am proud to have made a small contribution to your long-term financial success.*
>
> *Sincerely,*
> [*VBFP's Name*]

I also give away a lot of books because these can be the most meaningful gifts. One of the books I love to give is *The Winning Spirit*, which was published in association with the United States Olympic Committee and to which I contributed an essay.* The focus of the book is applying the qualities that distinguish Olympic athletes to the pursuits of our daily professional and personal lives. Excellence is a topic I know is important to all of my clients, and frequently I'd rather spend $15 on a book that can potentially change their lives than $25 on a clock that merely helps them know what time it is. Here's a note you might send with a book.

Please see the back of this book for more information on, or to place an order for, The Winning Spirit.

NOTE WITH BOOK

> *Dear* [*Client's/Prospect's Name*]:
> **The message in this book was meaningful for me. I hope you find it valuable for yourself or someone you care about.**
>
> **Warm regards,**
> [*VBFP's Name*]

Statement Review and More Referrals

The first statement review meeting continues to build trust with new clients. Schedule this meeting to coincide with the clients' receipt of their first statement of account. In this way, you position yourself again as a coach and teammate rather than as a salesperson. This meeting assures and confirms for clients that what you told them during the interview and presentation was more than just a selling technique. Continue to refer to their values at this meeting and each review meeting.

As you prepare for the statement review meeting, consider these six objectives.

1. Help your clients understand how to read and interpret their statements. (Clients who do not understand their statements tend to become uncomfortable and sometimes even suspicious.)

2. Update your clients about your progress with their referrals. (These are their relatives, friends and colleagues. Your clients will be interested in reactions and results.)

3. Now that their strategy has been implemented for several months, answer their questions and ask how they are feeling about it.

4. Acknowledge whatever they have done well in implementing their strategy.

5. Discuss whatever they are not doing well and obtain commitment about what they will do during the next three, six or nine months (before the next review). Remember, look for improvement not perfection.

6. Obtain more referrals. (Especially if the first statement indicates the long-term wisdom of your strategy or if you have had positive contacts with other referrals, clients will be even more willing to give other names to you.)

The statement review is mandatory in Values-Based Selling. Do whatever it takes to have this meeting. It separates the truly client-driven financial professionals from those who simply pay lip service to caring about their clients. If you are indeed a VBFP, this meeting is an important part of what you do because it demonstrates you care enough to coach and to hold your clients accountable for following up on their commitments to achieve their goals and fulfill their values.

The Nine Commandments of Maintaining Trust

Nine "commandments" can serve as guidelines for maintaining trust. If you follow these guidelines, the clients you want to keep will stay with you.

1. Do what you say you will do.
2. Underpromise and overdeliver.
3. Be honest.
4. Acknowledge mistakes quickly and offer a solution.
5. Be on time.
6. Call people as quickly with bad news as you would with good news.
7. Meet with clients several times per year.
8. Stick to your principles.
9. Always put your clients' interests ahead of your own.

Adding value consistently will help keep you in the forefront of your clients' minds and create what Ken Blanchard calls a "raving fan": someone who wants to tell friends about you. This is the subject of the next chapter: getting the Great Client referrals you need and deserve.

Summary

You are more than a financial professional; you contribute to the total quality of life of your clients by helping them achieve their goals and fulfill their core values.

Add value to your relationship with your clients by implementing these suggestions:

- Give the new client a welcome gift—perhaps a crystal clock or book.

- Systematically mail to new and existing clients one value-added piece each month. Each piece contains an idea that can contribute to some aspect of the client's health: mental, physical, relationship, spiritual or financial.

- Make sure you hold a statement review meeting to coincide with the first statement the client receives. This meeting confirms what you told the clients in the first interview and allows you to help them understand the statement, update them about your progress with their referrals, answer their questions, acknowledge what they have done well, discuss and obtain commitment for what they need to do better and elicit more referrals.

EXERCISE

Start looking for ideas for your value-added pieces now. Check newspapers, computer databases, industry periodicals and popular magazines. When you have found six you like, classify them into five categories: financial health, relationship health, mental health, physical health and spiritual health. Now find more until you have two or three articles for each category. After you have received permission to reprint the articles and decided on your own header design, you are ready to start sending value-added pieces to your clients—they will be very pleasantly surprised!

As you went through your sources, you may have found too many articles in one category or another. Keep a copy of each of these to start your value-added mailing system for referred prospects. We'll discuss this further in the next chapter. Obtain permission to reprint as necessary and set up your mailing system for referred prospects. These items should not be time dependent, so you can use the same eight every year.

Once you start looking for articles, you will start seeing new ones every place you look. That's good. Keep copies of these, too, and obtain permission to reprint them; you have now started collecting the 12 client mailing pieces you will need for next year!

NOTES

9. Achieve 100% Referrals: Your Great Clients Become Your Marketing Department.

Referrals are a natural by-product of Values-Based Selling. The high level of trust you've created opens the door, but you still must walk through it—and *ask* for those referrals. Your clients will provide referrals on the basis of two simple facts: 1) They trust you, and 2) they are impressed with your work. If you are not getting lots of referrals, your clients are sending you the message that either they do not trust you enough or they are not impressed by your work—or both. If you have been a needs salesperson, simply matching the right financial or insurance product with your clients' needs, this may explain a low rate of referrals. Even though you might be trusted, there is nothing too impressive about matching products with needs.

When asking for referrals, always emphasize how your client benefits. When you don't give your clients the opportunity to help you with referrals, you are doing them a disservice. Your referral process is only as strong as its weakest link, so follow these eight surefire steps.

1. **Ask in a way that shows the benefit to the clients.**

2. **Make it simple for your clients to provide referrals by being clear about what you want.**

3. **Have a place to write the names down.**

4. **Conduct research. Gather information about the person to whom you are being referred.**

5. **Build credibility with a good letter of introduction from the client to the referral.**

6. **Make value-added deposits to the referral's emotional bank account before you make contact (similar to what you learned in Chapter 8).**

7. **Make effective phone contact (see Chapter 10).**

8. **Don't sell on the phone. The purpose of the call is to find out if there's a reason to meet and see if there's potential for a business relationship.**

Show the Benefit to the Client.

To receive referrals easily, you need to ask for them reasonably. The following dialogue illustrates how effective it is for the Values-Based Financial Professional (VBFP) to explain the benefits and rationale of the referrals-based business before requesting referrals. The box at the end of the dialogue gives another option for the opening paragraph.

> **VBFP.** As my role in your life progresses, I will continue to help you achieve your financial goals and fulfill your values. Today, I have been your strategist in helping develop a realistic financial game plan. As time goes by, my job will be to make sure you continue to implement your strategy. I will also be your financial coach to be sure you stick with your strategy and to help you make adjustments if your situation changes. We are partners: you, me and all my other clients. We learn from each other.
>
> You have already achieved a great deal. You are one of the few who have taken charge of your finances. You have committed to a written financial strategy and have started to implement it. How do you feel about that?
>
> **Client.** I feel really good about it.

> **Remember:** *This strategy is only as effective as the trust you have built.*

VBFP.   Great! Many people don't realize that the most expensive and time-consuming part of being a financial professional is finding new clients. We often spend a substantial part of our time and effort in prospecting and marketing. This takes away from the time we can devote to the activities that make us better resources for our clients.

As my newest client, how would you rather I spend my time—looking for new clients, or thinking about your money and keeping an eye on issues that could affect your personal financial health?

Client.   I want you to think about my money.

VBFP.   Of course. And you're not alone. All my clients feel that way. For me to spend the time you want me to spend on looking after your financial best interests, I need your help. It is important for you and all my clients to help me keep my appointment calendar full by introducing me to people who meet my guidelines.

[*Handing client a description of ideal client.*] Here's a profile of the type of person I am looking for as a client. Let's talk about people you know who fit this profile.

The Lombardi/Cricket Approach

You can liven up your referrals conversation with interesting metaphors like this one that would substitute for the first paragraph of the previous dialogue.

VBFP: As my role in your life progresses, I will continue to help you achieve your financial goals and fulfill your values. Today, I have been your *strategist* in helping develop a realistic game plan. As time goes by, I'll become kind of a cross between Vince Lombardi and Jiminy Cricket. Lombardi, of course, was the great football coach. He was brilliant at getting the most out of his players. My job is to help you get the most out of your life by making smart choices about your money. And Jiminy Cricket was Pinocchio's conscience: He made sure Pinocchio did what he knew he ought to do. I'll ensure that you do what you ought to do in terms of saving for your future financial health. We are partners: you, me and all my other clients. We all help each other.

The Power of the Truth

Telling your clients that giving you referrals benefits them is not a gimmick; it is an honest disclosure. What if the increased number of referrals frees up ten hours per week? You can then spend five hours per week increasing your skills as a financial professional and take five hours more per week free time away from work. Both will make you a better resource for your clients.

In just five hours per week, you could take classes and read books and magazines about financial and insurance strategies. You could work on understanding your clients. It's amazing how little most financial professionals study financial success. Why don't they? Most simply don't have the time or energy to become great financial professionals because they spend all those hours and all that effort prospecting and marketing.

- Imagine how much better you will become when you study your craft five more hours each week.

- Imagine how much more relaxed and well balanced you will be when you take off five more hours each week.

One or both of these fantasies can come true if you allow your clients to do your prospecting and marketing for you. That five hours translates to 150–250 hours per year of improving your skill as a financial professional and 150–250 hours or more of free time for enhancing your own quality of life. Less stress and higher competence make you more valuable to your clients. How many years like this would it take for you to become the confident, centered, brilliant financial professional who *attracts* high-quality clients rather than pursuing them?

New clients trust you enough to tell you their values, disclose their assets and make a commitment to implement the strategy you recommend. They are honest with you, and they expect you to be honest with them. You've told them the truth about their financial situation, and they've reacted positively. Now, tell them the truth about the realities of your business. They will react positively again—and they will be eager to help you by introducing you to people you want to meet. It's in their best interest to help you.

Completing the Referral-Gathering Process

As the client provides you with names, write them on the referral sheet as shown on page 197. Notice that the sample list contains names only; there are no other details because you don't need to worry about the details until you have a whole list of names. Tell clients, "Write as many names as you can and just mail it back to me." Your goal is to obtain the names of more prospects than you can possibly see. Remember, the more names your clients give you, the more they help themselves. Freedom from prospecting and marketing benefits both you and your clients.

Expect clients to give you enough names to fill the referral sheet, and expect to complete the process. If you have 20 lines on the sheet and a client can come up with only seven names, photocopy the referral sheet for your files. Give your client the *incomplete* referral sheet (with only seven names) and say, "Don't worry about it. Many of my clients can't come up with 20 names off the top of their heads. I'll start with these seven. Feel free to take the sheet home, fill in as many more names as you can, and just mail it back to me."

After you have all the names the client can think of, you can proceed with preparing a questionnaire for each referral (see page 197). The questions shown can be included, and you probably will customize your questionnaire to suit your own style and type of business. The more you know about the referrals, the easier it will be to strike up a phone conversation with them so you can qualify them and set an appointment. Whatever questions you ask, take good notes.

Rules for Referrals

The following rules will help you develop your own referral profile and referral strategy.

1. Know important general facts about the people you want to be introduced to.

2. Be prepared to communicate to clients both verbally and in writing the type of person you are seeking.*

3. Have a place to write the names down.

4. Do some research. The more you know, the better.

5. Implement a simple value-added mail campaign to set the stage for your phone contact.

6. Determine exactly how you intend to conduct the phone conversation. Know what specific questions you will ask, and anticipate common concerns or reasons for not wanting to talk with you which the referred person might have.

7. Don't sell on the phone. The purpose of the call is to find out if there's a reason to meet and see if there's a potential for a business relationship.

8. Be a student of referrals. For more great information on how to be a master of referrals contact Mark Sheer at (949) 588–5931, or visit his website at www.marksheer.com.

---

* There is nothing more powerful than a client's endorsement of you in persuading a colleague, friend, or family member to consider working with you. An excellent accompaniment to their words of praise is a copy of *Values-Based Financial Planning,* a book I wrote to help demonstrate to financial consumers how valuable a trusted advisor, and the processes you are learning in this book, can be to them. This is far superior to a brochure or other promotional literature you might send along with clients who are recommending you to other people. Please refer to the back of this book for more information.

The Ideal Client Profile

Before you ask for referrals, you need to create an Ideal Client Profile. This description should be detailed and specific. The more precise it is, the more it will help you weed out prospects who will waste your time. The following is an example.

Sample Ideal Client Profile

- Is serious about personal financial success
- Has total household income of $75,000+
- Has net worth of $200,000+
- Owns home
- Cares for family, community, or someone or something other than self
- Has important financial goals
- Is receptive to professional relationships

Notice how the profile reflects a person who is already successful. Successful people make better clients for three reasons:

1. They recognize value.
2. They respect other successful professionals like you.
3. They have successful friends to introduce to you.

Referrals

Client Name _____

20. Name _____
19. Name _____
18. Name _____
17. Name _____
16. Name
15. Name
14. Name
13. Name
12. Name
11. Name
10. Name
9. Name
8. Name
7. Name
6. Name
5. Name
4. Name
3. Name
2. Name
1. Name

Sample Referral Questionnaire

Name: _____

Spouse: _____

Address: _____

Phone: _____

- What makes you think they are serious about achieving their financial goals?
- What are their occupations? Who are their employers?
- What are their ages?
- Do they have any children?
  Names: _____ Ages: _____
- Do they currently consult a financial professional?
- Have they ever discussed their financial goals or strategies for the future with you (e.g., retirement, college, vacation homes, vacations)? If yes, what have they told you?
- What type of clients do you think they'd be?
  - ❑ Great Client
  - ❑ Sometimes Worth Helping
  - ❑ Fun but Hopeless
  - ❑ Uses You for Information
  - ❑ Doesn't Trust Anybody

The last item on the Referral Questionnaire may seem strange, but it's a great way to avoid time wasters. Describe for your new clients the five client types (refer to Chapter 1), and tell them that they, of course, are Great Clients. Ask if they can identify the client type for each referral. After you have completed the referral questionnaire for each potential Great Client or Sometimes Worth Helping Client, thank your client and explain your usual procedure for contacting these new prospects:

VBFP. Thank you for your help.
I promise to contact these people
and deal with them in the same
professional manner I have dealt
with you.

It makes sense that we let these
referrals know I'm going to call
them. I don't expect you to call
all these people to tell them that,
so I've prepared a very simple
letter to accomplish that purpose.

[*Showing the letter.*] They will
receive this letter from you. I'll do
all the work. It's just like the one
you got from ——— when the
two of us were introduced.

If your new client was not referred to you,
part of the dialogue will be slightly different.
Simply change the third paragraph.

VBFP. They will receive this letter from
you. I'll do all the work preparing
and mailing the letter. All you'll
need to do is sign it.

The next thing I'll do is put them
on my value-added mailing list.
I like to send people information
that makes a positive difference in
their lives so they realize I'm not
just another financial salesperson—but that I really care and
want to help. I send them ideas of

value so they can experience my philosophy of business. This is the same kind of information I've been sending to you. I usually send one of these to each referral once a week. I try to provide items that will contribute to the person's physical, mental, spiritual, relationship and financial health.

Then, after a few weeks, I will call these people to discuss whether we have some basis for meeting. If so, I will make an appointment to meet them at their convenience. If not, that's OK, too.

[*Adding the following if it applies.*] My company also gives free financial seminars, so if they prefer I will invite them to a seminar. Some people are more comfortable getting to know us through seminars.

SAMPLE LETTER OF INTRODUCTION

Dear [*Referral Name*]:

I know you are always on the lookout for ideas that will help you achieve your financial goals and enhance your quality of life. With that in mind, I have asked my financial advisor, [*VBFP's full name*], to get in touch with you. [*VBFP's first name*] is my financial coach and is extremely professional. I feel my financial future is in much better shape as a result of working with [*VBFP's full name*]. Take some time to meet with [*him/her*] so you can decide for yourself if [*VBFP's first name*] can help you achieve your financial goals and enhance your quality of life.

Warm regards,

[*Client's Name*]

Send the Letter of Introduction.

Use the following guidelines to send the letter of introduction, which will create your referral's first impression about you. Obtain enough of your client's letterhead and envelopes, and have the letter printed on your laser-quality printer.

- Set an appointment with the client to sign the letters after you have printed them.

- Enter the referrals into your contact-management or database software.

- Merge the new referrals' names and addresses with the form letter and print out the letters and envelopes.

- Meet with the client to get signatures on the letters.

- Mail the letters.

- Print and stuff the value-added mailings for referrals so they arrive weekly after the letter from your client.

Special Note About Sending Introduction Letters

Resist the temptation to stuff the envelope full of promotional propaganda or even to insert a simple brochure. Let the strength of the relationship do the work for you. When you send propaganda, you appear to be just another product salesperson who needs business.

Value-Added Mailing Campaign for Referrals

This is basically the same approach as the value-added mail campaign outlined in Chapter 8. The primary difference is that for referrals you mail the pieces weekly for eight weeks instead of monthly for 12 months as you do for clients.

This means you will need to prepare another box for future mail, but this box will have dividers for each week. For each new referral, stamp and address eight envelopes, and insert two items:

1. A simple, brief cover letter on your letterhead, utilizing the strength of the referral.

2. One value-added piece.

Dear [*Referral's Name*]:

[*Client's Name*] **said you are always on the lookout for ideas to make smart financial choices and enhance your quality of life. That's why I have enclosed an idea that might make a difference. Feel free to call me if you want to discuss methods to achieve your highest level of success through the implementation of sound, long-term financial strategies.**

Warm regards,

[*VBFP's Name*]

The eight value-added pieces for referrals are different from the 12 pieces you send to clients because once the referrals become clients, they will be getting the client value-added pieces.

Go through the referral box every Monday morning, and mail one piece to each referral. When there is only one value-added piece left to be mailed to a specific referral, you know it is time to make the first phone contact. Call the referred prospects if they haven't already called you, and conduct the phone contact as explained in Chapter 10.

To ensure that you don't miss an opportunity, also put a reminder in your day planner or set the date in your contact-management software to call each referral during the seventh week of mailings. And remember: With Values-Based Selling, some referrals may call you before the seventh week. (This is one of the best benefits of the system.) In fact, when the system is in full swing, you will probably have only enough time to meet with the people who are calling you, and you will seldom have time to call the rest.

Your value-added mailings convey an attitude of caring and are consistent with the "soft" approach to prospecting and marketing referrals. You'll never get in trouble with your clients for selling their friends too hard. By mailing the eight pieces at weekly intervals, you are making "deposits into the emotional bank account." You haven't sent any promotional material or brochures; you have just sent the letter of introduction from the client and the value-added ideas. The phone contact itself does not include any selling. Rather, it is a discussion to see if there is a basis for you and the referral to meet.

May 15, 2001

Since writing this chapter in 1996 we received many, many requests for a simpler, turn-key system. The result is the *Values-Based Financial Planning Book* and monthly *Newsletter* program. For a more detailed description and pricing for the *Values-Based Financial Planning Book* and *Newsletter* see the promotional information in the back of the book.

By waiting to make contact until the referrals have received several mailings or by letting them call you prior to the seventh week, you avoid being perceived as needing the business. People prefer to work with professionals who are successful and not needy.

Even the referral who does not do business with you will think of you in a positive way. If you decide certain referrals are qualified and you would really like to do business with them, but the timing wasn't right to meet with them during the eight-week referral campaign, keep them in the loop and send them your monthly pieces for the rest of the year. This is a great way to maintain contact and make more deposits until the timing is right.

Maintain an Expectant Attitude.

Since you know giving referrals benefits both the client and you, *expect* your clients to provide introductions. Ask for referrals with the same confident approach you use in the rest of the client development process. When financial professionals don't get referrals, there are several negative consequences:

Client development *not* based on referrals is expensive. Prospecting and marketing cost you more to get the prospects into your office, more per appointment, and more per client. Moreover, the percentage of these more expensive prospects who become Great Clients will be smaller than with referred prospects.

Client development *not* based on referrals is time-consuming. You must have more clients to generate the additional income needed both for marketing and for the net income you want. The more clients you have, the less service and time you can give to each one. Time-consuming prospecting prevents you from becoming a great financial professional, which in turn shortchanges all your clients. Traditional sales training advocates that you tolerate a good deal of rejection. I disagree. Instead, I suggest you become so skilled that you don't get much rejection.

Client development *not* based on referrals is mentally exhausting. Prospecting and marketing are the most draining aspects of the financial services business. Whatever affects your mental sharpness also affects the quality of the advice and service you give to your clients.

For more sample dialogues for requesting referrals, see Appendix D. But remember that your clients won't make referrals based on your smooth execution of a script—the referral process is closely tied to all that happened earlier in the client development process. Ultimately, *everything* hinges on the trust you built with your client in the first five minutes.

- You have clients who are doing your prospecting and marketing for you because you put together an accurate, compelling strategy that greatly impressed them.

- Your clients are committed to implementing your strategy because it was well prepared, and it represents their deepest values and ultimate goals.

- You prepared so well because you found out what their financial goals are and where all their money is.

- You experienced a thorough, honest discovery because you earned clients' trust with the values conversation.

- **Therefore, you are getting referrals easily now because of what occurred during the first five minutes of the first interview with each client.**

Referrals are a measure of the quality of the relationship between the VBFP and the client. All success can be traced back to client trust. Nothing works without it. And you can now create it on purpose every time.

Values-Based
Client Development Cycle

Phone Contact
You are brilliant on the phone with warm, referred leads which position you for a great . . .

Interview
The values conversation creates trust which facilitates honest and complete financial disclosure, enabling you to prepare an impressive . . .

First Statement Review
Continued, sincere interest in clients' health leads to more referrals and eventual . . .

Strategy
Only a compelling and accurate strategy will be implemented upon . . .

Value-Added Campaign
Regular, meaningful contact maintains and builds more trust until . . .

Presentation
Because your clients trust you completely and are impressed with your work, they implement your recommendations and provide referrals. Your clients and their referrals benefit from the . . .

How to Ask for Referrals From Existing Clients

Go through your files and identify only the Great Clients. Set up meetings to tell them about your business plan. Use the two sample dialogues below to guide you in requesting referrals from them.

REFERRAL REQUEST #1

VBFP. As you may know, cold-calling, direct mail, prospecting, networking and many other methods of marketing are expensive and time-consuming. I've recently realized that I want more clients just like you. I have a goal. In order to achieve it, I need 25 new good clients. I'm asking good clients like you to help me out.

[*Showing the Ideal Client Profile.*] Here is the type of new client I'm looking for.

REFERRAL REQUEST #2

VBFP. We've been doing business for some time now, and you're an excellent client. What you might not know about my business is that when I have to spend a lot of time on prospecting and marketing for new clients, it takes away from the time I can invest in staying on top of the issues

People love to help one another. Let your clients help you succeed.

and trends that impact your financial life. I've made a commitment to change this, and you can help me. Would you be willing to do that?

Client. Of course.

VBFP. Great. I'm always looking for new ways to be more valuable to you. You know exactly the kind of people who could perhaps benefit from a relationship with me. You already have good experience working with me.

[*Showing the Ideal Client Profile.*] Here's a profile of the people I want to work with. Who do you know who meets these criteria?

REFERRALS FOR THE ASKING

"Since your program, I've asked two of my top 20 clients for referrals. This was totally outside my comfort zone. With the first client, I was less prepared and talked too much and still got results. When I talked with the second client, I handed him the qualities of a 'welcomed referral' and I'm going to get 8–10 great referrals.

"Your program is so process-oriented that I couldn't help but try it, and now I've overcome a fear of asking for referrals."

CAROL CLEMENTS
Money Concepts

Bachrach & Associates is 100% referral-based. Indeed, my clients want me to spend my time researching ideas that will help me teach them how to succeed at their highest level, rather than prospecting for new business. Wouldn't your clients want the same of you? Of course, once you have the referrals you need, you must maximize the first phone contact. How? Read on . . .

Summary

- Clients who trust the VBFP and are impressed with the work will gladly provide referrals.
- Here are eight guidelines that will help you obtain referrals and turn the referred prospects into lifetime clients:

1. Ask for referrals in a way that shows clients how they stand to benefit from giving you referrals.

2. Make it simple for your clients to provide referrals by showing them your Ideal Client Profile.

3. Write down the names as your clients provide them.

4. Research: Find out as much as you can from your client about the referred prospect.

5. Build credibility with the referred prospect by sending a good letter of introduction from the client to the referral.

6. Send seven or eight value-added mailing pieces to the referral before you make contact.

7. Decide exactly what you will say before you call. Anticipate common concerns.

8. Don't sell on the phone; just try to determine if there is a reason to meet and if there is a potential for a good business relationship.

- By building a referral-based business you avoid the expense, time and mental effort involved in cold-marketing and prospecting.

- By building a referral-based business you give yourself more time to become a better person and a better VBFP for your clients.

EXERCISE

Using the guidelines in this chapter and the dialogues in Appendix D, choose three of your Great Clients and call them to ask for referrals. Tell them you're trying a new technique to improve the value you can give to them and your other clients. Explain how giving you referrals benefits them. Expect them to give you great referrals, and they will give you great referrals.

NOTES

_____

_____

_____

_____

_____

_____

_____

_____

_____

_____

_____

_____

_____

_____

_____

_____

_____

_____

_____

_____

_____

_____

_____

_____

_____

_____

_____

_____

_____

10. Be Brilliant on the Phone!

Suppose I were to call you right now and say, "I understand you are a successful financial professional who is always on the lookout to do the best possible job for your client and to achieve your highest level of success. Is that right?" What would you say? If my information was accurate, you would say, "Of course," and I would have a basis for a continuing conversation and perhaps a meeting. If you responded negatively, I would quickly identify that you were not a good prospect for me and end the call. This is the purpose of a good phone contact: to capture the interest of the right people and quickly let the wrong ones go.

Your receptivity to any phone call is directly related to the accuracy and depth of information your caller has about you. For example, how receptive are you when the caller can't even pronounce your name?

NEVER OPEN THE CALL WITH YOUR NAME AND COMPANY.

I know that what I'm suggesting is contrary to what your mother, your manager and the sales trainer have taught you about being polite on the phone. You are supposed to introduce yourself and company immediately. But what's so polite about starting with something your prospects don't care about, won't remember, and might put them on the defensive? This is why the information you got from your client about the referral is so crucial. It allows you to open the conversation with something they do care about. That's what being client-focused is all about!

It is crucial to avoid selling in the first phone contact with a prospect. If you don't try to sell anything, you don't give the prospect anything to say no to. And, if you have done your research as suggested in the last chapter, you will be able to ask your prospects questions to which you know they will answer yes, assuming they are Great Clients or Sometimes Worth Helping.

One key to success lies in your ability to convert phone contact with qualified prospects to appointments in which you obtain full financial disclosure and a precommitment to create a financial strategy. Use the emotional pull of the values conversation and the logical push of a cohesive, written financial strategy to ensure that you will turn qualified prospects into Great Clients.

The Phone Dialogue With a Referral

This sample phone dialogue illustrates how to use what you already know about the person you're contacting to spark an interest in talking with you.

Shawn. [*Answering the phone.*] Hello.

VBFP. Hello, is this Shawn Prospect?

Shawn. Yes.

VBFP. [*Leading with the referror's name—not his/her own.*] Hi, Shawn. Terry Client asked me to call you, and I promised I would. Terry said you are always on the lookout for

215

ideas that help you achieve your financial goals and enhance your quality of life. Is that true?

Shawn. Yes.

VBFP. Because that's what I do for a living, Terry thought you and I should talk.

[*Introducing self now, at a point when the prospect cares.*] My name is [*VBFP's Name*]. Terry mailed you a letter about me, and for the past few weeks I have been sending you some ideas designed to improve your quality of life. Sound familiar?

Shawn. Oh, yeah. Some of those ideas were pretty good.

VBFP. I'm glad you liked them. Now, just because I was able to help Terry doesn't mean I can be of value to you, but we can figure that out pretty quickly. I'm not calling to sell you anything, just to see if we should consider getting together. Is now a good time to talk for a few minutes?

If the prospect says yes, proceed as below. If the prospect says no, set a phone appointment, and during the subsequent call continue the discussion as follows.

VBFP. Since you and I don't know each other, I need to understand a few things about you to help us determine if it makes sense for us to get together.

[*Using the information from the Ideal Client Profile.*] I tend to work with people who are serious about personal financial success, earn more than $75,000 per year, have a net worth of at least $200,000, own a home, care about something other than themselves, have important financial goals and are receptive to professional relationships. How much of that description fits you?

Shawn. Most of it.

VBFP. The first step in helping people make intelligent choices about their money is to understand the importance of money to them. Help me understand, what's important about money *to you*?

Proceed with the values conversation as described in Chapter 2, confirm that the prospect has named the highest core value, then continue as follows:

VBFP. [*Restating the prospect's values in his own words.*] Suppose we were able to create a very specific written strategy that helps you make smart financial choices so you can ———. Would that give us a basis for working together, from your perspective?

Shawn. Yes, it would.

VBFP. From my perspective, you sound like the type of person I can help to make smart financial choices, and who can benefit from a working relationship with me. There is no charge for an initial consultation. I have some time available in my calendar next week. Which day is best for you and your wife?

Shawn. How about next Tuesday, 10–11 A.M.?

VBFP. That will be fine. I'm going to send you a list of documents to bring. These include every single paper that indicates anything about your current financial situation, things like tax returns, brokerage account statements, mutual fund statements and bank statements. Is there any reason that would prevent you from bringing those documents with you next Tuesday morning?

If the prospect says "No problem," proceed as follows.

VBFP. Fine, then I'll send you the list and I'll see you and your wife next Tuesday.

However, if the prospect says he cannot get all the documents together for your appointment, proceed as follows.

Shawn. Let me think. No, I can't possibly get all that stuff together before Tuesday, but can we meet then anyway?

VBFP. We really need the documents to accomplish anything meaningful. How much time do you need to gather them?

Shawn. I'm sure I can have all the documents by a week from Tuesday.

VBFP. OK, great. I've got my calendar in front of me. What time is good for you on that day?

And if the prospect resists bringing the documents to the first meeting at all, proceed this way.

Shawn. I'm not sure I'm ready to tell you all about my finances yet, so I don't want to bring my financial documents to this meeting.

VBFP. I understand. Whether you work with me or end up working with another financial professional, if you are sincere about getting a handle on your financial life, you'll have to get your financial documents together. They are crucial to creating an effective financial strategy. Showing me your financial documents is not the first thing you'll do when we get together. First we'll get to know more about each other. You need to be comfortable with me and we both need to decide if we have a basis for working together.

Go ahead and get your financial documents together and bring them with you. You can leave them in your briefcase, put them in a paper bag or leave them in your car if you like. But you must have them with you. It won't take us long to determine if we should proceed or not. If you do not bring your documents, we will have to set another appointment. That wouldn't be a very good use of your time or mine. Bring the documents. If you don't want to show them to me, we'll end the meeting there. If you do want my help, we can make good progress. Does that sound reasonable to you?

Shawn.   Yes.

VBFP.   OK. I'll see you on Tuesday at 10.

This is a reasonable, professional approach. If it doesn't seem reasonable to your prospect, then you are dealing with an unreasonable person. The time to discover unreasonableness is as early as possible—and don't meet with the person.

Next, send a letter (see sample on page 222) that confirms the appointment. Emphasize the prospect's own values (if you conducted the values conversation over the phone), and include a list of what the prospect should bring to the meeting. Do not send any promotional material, brochures or propaganda. Send only the letter, your business card, a map to your office, and the document list.

Other than knowing their values, how do you know from a phone conversation whether prospects are reasonable people? First, certain factual details will help you make this judgment. Pay attention to how they answer the question about being on the lookout for ideas to achieve financial goals, what they respond to when you share your ideal client profile and how willing they are to engage in the values conversation. Much of your decision will be based on the subjective feeling you have about the conversation. Are they interested in what you have to say and to offer? Or are they honestly skeptical about financial professionals but at least willing to listen? Both of these are indications of a promising client. Or do they put up smoke screens at every turn and go out of their way to avoid meeting with you? If they are determined not to meet with you, let them win.

LETTER TO SEND AFTER SETTING AN APPOINTMENT

Dear Shawn Prospect:

I enjoyed our conversation on the phone, and I look forward to meeting with you and your wife, Sheila, next Tuesday at 10 A.M. to further discuss how you can make smart choices about your money and enhance your quality of life. A lot of insurance agents and investment people might make that same claim, but I'm talking about the smart choices that give you freedom of choice, giving you the opportunity to do what you want, ultimately making a meaningful impact on the world.

Enclosed is a list of documents for you to bring to our first meeting. These documents will be necessary to ascertain what will be the best course of action for you. If you have any questions, please feel free to give me a call.

Sincerely,

[VBFP's Name]
Enclosures: Directions to the Office
               Document List
               Business Card

Notice how the letter includes Shawn's values. Be sure to include your prospects' values in their letters.

Questions to Make Prospects Think and to Create Curiosity

The following dialogue can be used during a phone contact to motivate reluctant prospects to meet you if you don't want to let them go without another try.

VBFP.   Would you mind if I ask you a question?

Prospect.   No.

VBFP.   Will your current written financial strategy bridge the gap between where you are now and where you want to be?

Prospect.   My strategy is not in writing.

VBFP.   OK, then perhaps I can help you. But I can't be sure you need my services because I don't know enough about you and your financial situation. By the same token, you don't know enough about who I am and what I do to be sure that I can't help either. The only way we can both find out is by having a meeting. I have some time available next week. Which day works best for you?

Below is a list of questions the Values-Based Financial Professional (VBFP) can ask to further encourage the prospect to set an appointment. Refer to Appendix E for more sample dialogues. If you've had sales training in "disturbing" clients and backing them into a corner, be careful that you don't come across as snide or sarcastic. Instead, communicate with genuine curiosity and a sincere desire to help.

- "Do you have a coach who helps you make smart financial choices on a regular basis? Or do you just have people who sell you stuff occasionally? Does the idea of a financial coach appeal to you?"

- "Have you ever thought about how smart it would be to have a written Financial Road Map?"

- "If you do not have a written financial strategy yet, has it occurred to you that maybe this phone call isn't a coincidence? Many things do not happen by accident. Maybe it's finally time for you to define your financial strategy in writing. I can help you with that. What do you think?"

- "Is it possible that one reason you do not have a written financial strategy is that nobody has shown you how to create one?"

- "Fewer than 5% of the people in our country are on track to be financially independent by the time they are in their sixties. Remarkably, a large number of the 95% who are not on track seem to think they are. What about you? Do you know you are on track to be financially independent, or is it possible you are part of the 95% who aren't sure? Would you like to know for sure?"

- "Most people's investments can be described as a hodgepodge of diverse investments, insurance policies and bank accounts that don't work together. They've been accumulated at random over many years. Is this how you've purchased your investments, or were they purchased to work in harmony toward achieving your goals?"

- "If you were ever going to create a written financial strategy, when would be the best time to do that?"

- "Have you ever noticed which athletes have coaches? That's right: The best always have coaches. What about you? Would you like to find out what it's like to have a financial coach who helps you chart a course toward financial independence and then helps you implement your strategy over time?"

These questions might move an initially reluctant Great Client to meet with you. But don't push too hard or you'll end up setting appointments with the wrong people. You are better off prospecting for the right clients than having appointments with the wrong ones.

The First Meeting: After You Have Had the Values Conversation on the Phone

The values conversation is just as effective on the telephone as in person. If you identified your prospect's values from a phone conversation, you can begin immediately with discovery at your first face-to-face meeting.

If you are meeting with a couple, first conduct the values conversation with the spouse whose values you haven't yet explored. (See Appendix A, "How to Conduct the Values Conversation with Couples.")

When preparing for this meeting, write your prospect's values on the WIA ——— TY staircase. Make it available for your prospect to see during the following dialogue. Then the first face-to-face meeting with the client will go like this.

VBFP. When we spoke on the phone, Shawn, you shared with me that making smart choices about money is important so you can have freedom of choice, giving you the opportunity to do what you want, ultimately making a meaningful impact on the world. Is that right?

Shawn. Yes.

VBFP. Is there anything you would like to add or clarify before we proceed?

Shawn. No, that's about it.

VBFP. Terrific. Suppose we're able to create a strategy that will enable you to make smart choices about your money so you can enjoy these things you've told me are important to you. Would that give us a basis for doing business?

Shawn. Yes, it would.

VBFP. Now that we are clear about what's important to you, the next step is for us to be equally clear about the details of your current financial situation and your financial goals. Where would you like to begin, with your goals or with your current financial situation?

Listen and follow your prospects' lead regarding where they would like to begin. Put the WIA ——— TY staircase away for now and fill in the details in the confidential questionnaire and Financial Road Map, as described in Chapter 5.

Points to Remember About Phone Contact

Successful people are your target market, and they tend to look for ways to minimize interruptions to their lives. It's understandable for them to try to dismiss at first someone they may perceive as a salesperson. **Persisting politely and asking the right questions**

effectively will convey your belief in what you do and will build curiosity so they want to meet with you. As you make the transition from salesperson to VBFP, this should become easier and easier.

When you call "warm referrals," review the following points to strengthen your telephone skills:

- Expect a positive response to your call, but be prepared for an initially negative one. Not everyone will jump at the chance to meet with you. You want to move smoothly into the questions that will give them a clear reason to agree to an appointment or to show their true colors.

- Use the values conversation on the phone to give your prospect emotional reasons—trust—to meet with you.

- Include the prospect's values in the confirmation letter to increase the emotional commitment to the appointment and to decrease the chance of cancellation.

- Focus. Sell the process of financial strategizing and making smart financial decisions. (Do not sell one product or service over the phone.)

- Remember that many people who have a "financial professional" in their lives do not have a written financial strategy. The fact that you help people create written strategies and make intelligent financial choices based on a sound strategy can get your foot in a door that will be closed to more traditional stockbrokers or insurance agents.

- Preparation, once again, is crucial. If you have a poor contact-to-appointment conversion ratio, it's probably because you have not prepared well enough. Use the information your client has given you to help qualified prospects understand why they should meet with you.

Now, with a great value-added campaign, 100% referrals and an unstoppable phone presence, you are perfectly positioned to take your business reputation to the next level—*celebrity*. The next chapter tells you precisely how.

Summary

For successful, brilliant phone contacts, follow these guidelines:

1. Do your research. From the Referral Questionnaire filled out with the help of your client, you should have enough information about the referred prospect that you can comfortably customize the phone conversation.
2. Don't introduce yourself until the prospect has a reason to care who you are.
3. If the prospect does not have the time to talk with you when you call, set a specific time and date for a five- to ten-minute phone conversation.
4. Don't give the prospect anything to say no to; through your research, you should already know that the answers to your first questions will be yes.

5. Don't sell on the phone.

6. To determine if this prospect is "in" or "out," conduct the values conversation during the phone call. It will help both of you determine whether you have a reason to meet.

7. Once you have conducted the values conversation, use the emotional pull of the prospect's values as the reason to meet with you.

8. Set a specific time and date for an appointment.

9. Make sure the prospect can and will bring all the financial documents to the meeting. If the prospect cannot get the documents together by the specified date, reschedule the appointment for a date when all the documents will be available so you can obtain complete financial discovery.

10. Send a follow-up letter that mentions the prospect's values, confirms the date and time of the meeting and includes a list of documents that the prospect is to bring to the meeting.

11. If you meet resistance on the phone, ask one or two of the questions on pages 224 and 225 of this chapter to motivate the prospect or use one of the dialogues suggested in Appendix E.

EXERCISE

Call one of the prospects on your current list. If this is not a referred prospect, change the dialogue accordingly. Instead of saying "Hi, Shawn. Terry Client asked me to call you . . . Terry said you were always on the lookout for ideas that help you achieve your financial goals and enhance your quality of life," say this: "Hi, Shawn. I understand that you are a person who is always on the lookout for ideas that can help you achieve your financial goals and enhance your quality of life." Proceed from there to conduct the values conversation and to set an appointment. If you meet resistance, ask one or two of the questions on pages 224 and 225 of this chapter to motivate the prospect or try using one of the dialogues suggested in Appendix E. (Go ahead—you have nothing to lose.)

NOTES

_____

_____

_____

_____

_____

_____

_____

_____

11. Become a Celebrity in Your Target Market.

In financial services, there's no one road to stardom. To become a celebrity in your target market, you can choose one or more of the routes suggested in this chapter. By all means, take the path on which you are most comfortable. But be aware that the more of these steps you take, the more quickly and effectively you will achieve celebrity status.

Here are some strategies that can help propel you along the path to stardom.

Write a Book on Making Smart Financial Choices, Specifically for Your Target Market.

This is not as difficult as you may think. Remember, you don't have to reinvent the principles of financial success. There are certain fundamentals everyone needs to know. Then you can teach others the philosophies and techniques you have developed in your work with clients. Your book will combine those principles and your philosophy—all in your own words. The research must be factual, but your philosophy is your opinion and is what makes the book unique. Don't underestimate the power of a book that has your name on it—either as author or coauthor.

Writing a book is not easy, but it's doable. Chances are the simplest path is to self-publish your book. There are many resources that can help you self-publish. Several are listed in the bibliography at the back of this book. I especially recommend the books by Dan Poynter, Tom and Marilyn Ross and Gordon Burgett. The people who helped me with this book are listed in the front of it.

Considerations to Keep in Mind When Writing a Book

1. Write about an area in which you have expertise.
2. Address the issues that are currently relevant to your market.
3. Target the book very narrowly and specifically so that the people you want to reach will immediately see that it is of interest to them.

Revisions to update or customize a book are usually much easier than writing the first edition. People continue to be impressed by each revision or separate edition you put out for each specific target market. Having your book published gets your clients' egos cooking: "My financial coach wrote a book!"

What a great way to get referrals! Show your new clients your Ideal Client Profile, ask them for referrals and tell them, "I want to send each of these people a free, autographed copy of my book with your compliments." Sending a book is much better than sending a brochure or other promotional literature and is a great enhancement to your value-added mail campaign for referrals.

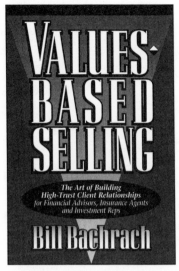

Notice that the name of this book indicates my area of expertise; addresses a topic very relevant to you, my target market; and specifies my target audience.

Subscribe to the Publications Your Target Market Reads.

The professional association for your target market probably has at least one and possibly many publications, ranging from fairly sophisticated magazines to desktop-published newsletters. Build a relationship with the editors of these publications so they will invite you to participate as an author or as a member of the editorial board.

I certainly can't read everything in all 30-plus publications my office receives, but someone on my staff looks through each of them and points out to me articles of interest. We discover articles about our target-market decision makers, people who may or may not be clients yet. We may clip an article and send it to them, or write to them about the article. This is powerful because it tells our clients and potential clients that we noticed. Also, through such articles we learn more about those decision makers—information that will help us when we do get referred to them.

This familiarity with leading figures and current issues in your target market gives you a lot of confidence dealing with your prospects. You not only know your business, you also know a lot about *their* business. (One of the most valuable skills you can have as a financial professional is the ability to have an understanding of someone's business without having that person's biases or limitations.)

Write Articles for Publications That Give Specific Financial Advice for Your Target Market.

To find out which publications are best for your articles, read each journal's mission statement and author guidelines. Often the editors are happy to receive articles giving financial advice written specifically for their readers. (They usually do not pay for them, but they might.) Check the masthead in the front of the publication to see if it lists a finance editor. If it doesn't, volunteer to be one!

I've published about 50 articles in the last four years in financial services publications. Because of this, you may have recognized my name when you saw this book. In fact, it may even have motivated you to buy it. The same strategy will work for you.

Get Involved.

Join the local and national professional associations to which your target clients belong. For example, I belong to the General Agents and Managers Association, the National Association for Life Underwriters, and the International Association of Financial Planning, although I am no longer licensed in these fields. Because I am a professional speaker and consultant for the financial services profession, these associations give me professional connections to my clients and keep me up to date with what is happening in the industry.

If you become involved in professional societies relevant to your target market, you may be asked to speak at meetings or contribute articles. All these activities give you the name recognition that is the beginning of celebrity.

Obviously, then, it is important to contribute to those meetings in whatever way you can. For example, not only do I contribute my speaking services to industry events, but I also make monetary contributions to the foundations and research programs. Why? Because I want to give something back to the industry that has given so much to me, and because I want it to succeed. Just as your success depends on your clients' success, my success depends on the success of the financial services industry, my target market. I want our industry to be able to finance the market research that will allow it to succeed at the highest levels, and I want the information that comes from that research so I can make the biggest possible contribution.

You can also contribute to associations by volunteering to serve on committees such as a membership committee, program committee, or a welcoming committee. By all means, get involved in the association. But don't try to sell anything to other members right away. First get to know the decision makers. Prove that you are a contributing member with a genuine interest in the organization. If other members ask why you belong, simply say, "I am a financial professional. I believe in what you do, and I'm considering making this a market that I specialize in. At this point, I don't even want to try to sell my services here because I don't understand enough about who you are and what you do. I'm really just here to learn about you." What an impression!

Resist the temptation to sell anything, because the association members have probably already had experiences with financial professionals who joined the association just to pitch their services and never contributed anything. Show that you are different, and you're on your way to making great contacts who will help you understand that market.

Capitalize on the Information You Get From Professional Meetings and Society Publications.

You can sometimes get association publications, a great source of information, without being qualified for membership in the organization. For example, an important organization for me is the Million Dollar Round Table (MDRT). I have spoken several times at the annual meeting of this prestigious insurance organization. I wanted to keep up with their research and what they were doing, but I assumed their publication, *Round the Table,* was only for MDRT members. I was wrong. After obtaining an edition for us to review, one of my staff members simply took out the subscription reply card and filled it out. She checked the nonmember box and sent them a check. Now we get the magazine. I wonder how many insurance agents are unaware that they can subscribe to this magazine that might help them qualify for MDRT?

This is just one example of how accessible various kinds of information about your target market can be if you just pay attention. The information is out there—information that can keep you up to date on the issues important to your client target market. Find the sources and use the information to become more credible in your market.

Become a Good Public Speaker.

If you enjoy speaking and have worked on developing this skill, you can offer to give seminars for professional organizations that represent your target markets. Volunteer for the planning committee for the annual convention, and suggest that they consider offering a seminar on a topic such as managing your money, managing your cash flow or creating an effective business plan. If they like the idea (and they usually will), volunteer to present the seminar! Prepare and present your material well, and you'll impress the association members who attend the seminar.

So how do you become an impressive speaker?

- Give a lot of speeches to become comfortable in front of an audience.
- Join a local chapter of Toastmasters International or enroll in a Dale Carnegie course.
- Hire a coach.
- Rehearse and videotape your presentations. Ask friends, colleagues and associates for feedback.
- Commit to becoming a good speaker. Establish goals and milestones, and follow through on your commitment.
- Remain open to feedback and coaching, no matter how successful you become.

Research and Interview
the Most Respected People
in Your Target Market.

Talking to these people helps you understand your target market better and build relationships with important individuals who can introduce you to others.

Understanding your market and the people in it is crucial to Values-Based Selling. Don't you hate it when someone approaches you and tries to sell you something without knowing anything about you? Talking to key people will put you in position to discover current concerns, hot issues and their unique perspectives about what's going on in their industry. High-trust, long-term relationships are based on making the extra effort to be informed.

When we call to interview executives and producers prior to a meeting for which they have hired me to speak, we get a very positive response. Most speakers don't call to interview anyone before the program. This extra effort adds to my credibility and keeps me in touch with events and trends in the industry, as well as at this company.

Get to know those people who will provide you with introductions to other key people. Within a few years you will be in a very unique referral position. For example, at Bachrach & Associates we seldom use a client profile to ask for referrals anymore. We now show our best clients a list of names and companies to whom we want to be introduced. Because we understand our business well, we can say to our best clients, "We want to do business with ——— company, and ——— is the decision maker there. Do you know this person? Would you call him/her for us and arrange a phone conversation?" Our clients introduce us to the person we want to meet. Of course, this only works if you know exactly who you want to talk to. The smaller and tighter your market, the easier it is to become well known.

You will end up earning trust by association. Prospects will say to you, "Oh, you're Terry's financial advisor? Wow, if he thinks you do good work, you must be doing good work!" Your credibility is established, and your contacts will continue to provide you with referrals who will in turn provide you with other referrals. Soon, you have a referral-based business that started with people at the top—and you have a lot of Great Clients because of it.

A VBFP Understands a Client's Business.

Consider this story I heard from one of my clients.

A dentist had an appointment with an insurance agent he was pretty skeptical about. The agent arrived at the dentist's office in a flashy Porsche, which of course did not impress the dentist at all. But the dentist changed his tune completely when he learned the agent could name every piece of equipment in the office, clearly understood the financial and business challenges of dentists and quickly got down to business to discover what this dentist was all about. Not only did the agent have just about every other well-respected dentist in that community as a client, he clearly cared about this dentist. The dentist told my client, "When that guy drove away, I had a totally different perspective than when he drove up. It was clear to me I was dealing with a very successful guy, and I understood why." The Values-Based Financial Professional who thoroughly understands the client's profession gains a well-earned reputation among other professionals.

Get Testimonials From People Who Think You're Wonderful.

The first step in getting testimonials is to ask for them. Next, you can ask three specific questions, the answers to which become the basis for the testimonial letter:

- What did you expect to get when you first met with me?
- What did you actually get?
- What have been the results of our relationship?

The outcome of these pointed questions is often a letter like the one below.

SAMPLE TESTIMONIAL LETTER

Dear VBFP:

I wanted to take a few moments to tell you about how important our work together has been to me. When we first met, I expected you to be just another person who would try to sell me financial and insurance products. What happened was that you helped me create a vision of my financial future. You have been an invaluable coach along the way to implementing my financial strategy. As a result of our relationship, I feel totally confident about my ability to provide for my family, have the quality of life I want, and enjoy the things that are important to us. Thank you so much for your help!

Warm regards,
Terry Client

Improve Your Target Marketing Skills.

I do not claim to be a teacher of target marketing, but I have been a good student and implementer. I haven't tried to tell you what your specific market is, because I know that people with many different target markets will read this book. What I have tried to do, however, is to illustrate how a clearly defined target market and the effective implementation of a focused strategy can shorten the time it takes to have a financial services practice that is simple, profitable and propels you rapidly toward your goals and fulfilling your values.

My personal belief is that the better you define your target market, the better job you will do for the lifetime clients you develop. When you narrow your market effectively, you will earn more money in less time because you work only with Great Clients who trust you with all their assets.

If you need to know more about target marketing methods, look to the leaders in this area, like Steve Moeller and Richard Weylman. For help in maintaining your focus on the best possible clients I recommend Dan Sullivan's "Strategic Coach" focusing program.*

By using Values-Based Selling, you can choose only the Great Clients and sell to them consistently and effectively. But *mastery* is the key to transforming what are now just words in a book into skills that are yours.

You can contact Steve Moeller at (800) 678-1701, Richard Weylman at (800) 535-4332 and The Strategic Coach at (800) 387-3206.

Summary

Being a celebrity in your target market means you will be sought for advice and prospects will recognize your name as soon as you say it. Here are eight possible routes to stardom in your target market.

1. Write a book on making smart financial choices, specifically for your target market.

2. Subscribe to the same publications your target market reads and volunteer to participate in those publications (e.g., as financial editor).

3. Write articles for the publications to give specific financial advice to your target market.

4. Get involved with the local and national professional associations to which people in your target market belong.

5. Capitalize on the information you obtain from professional meetings and publications.

6. Become a good public speaker and give brilliant presentations about financial advice at the professional meetings attended by people in your target market.

7. Research and interview the most respected people in your target market to discover their specific concerns, issues and unique perspectives.

8. Get testimonials from the people who think you're wonderful.

EXERCISE

Today, call one of your Great Clients who is a member of your target market. Ask the questions below, and take good notes during the conversation. Then decide which of the eight routes to stardom you will pursue first. Then pursue it!

Ask these questions of your target-market client:

1. What professional publications do you subscribe to?

2. If you had unlimited funds, are there any other professional publications to which you would subscribe?

3. What professional organizations do you belong to?

4. If you had unlimited funds, are there any other professional organizations to which you would belong?

5. Is there an elite organization that you and your colleagues all strive for membership in?

6. Who would you say are the five most respected people in your profession?

7. Do you know of any books on financial advice specifically written for people in your field? If so, what are they, and who wrote them?

NOTES

12. Mastery or Modification: To Change or Not to Change?

Fact: Thinking about exercising will not make you physically fit.

Fact: Thinking about implementing the ideas in this book will not make you a Values-Based Financial Professional (VBFP).

Everyone who reads this book, listens to my tapes or hears me speak has to make a choice. Are they going to master Values-Based Selling, let it slide and do nothing, or make some attempt to modify it? **The best results come from mastery.**

Mastering Values-Based Selling calls on you to make a change. Old-school sales training taught you to

- build a little rapport through superficial chitchat or small talk;
- explain yourself, your credentials and your company;
- ask some questions to uncover the need or "disturb" the prospect;
- match products to needs;
- explain the features and benefits of products;
- use fear or greed to move clients emotionally;
- handle objections;
- close.

The old school teaches that the key to success is prospecting and activity—forever. Now I've come along and contradicted all that. The old school is selling by accident. It's impersonal. It creates all the wrong emotions. It undermines building high-trust relationships. It takes way too long. And it doesn't position you for referrals. It might be OK for selling copiers, but it's sure not the way to earn trust, get people to give you all their money and introduce you to everyone they know who meets your criteria. Chances are that in your heart and your gut you know it's true. You have probably always been uncomfortable with some of the tactics you have used to sell people your products, but either you didn't know what else to do or you rationalized, "The end justifies the means."

Instead, I'm telling you to do the following:

- Eliminate all small talk and chitchat and open the interview with the meaningful and emotional values conversation. (Some prospects might even cry.) Meaningful human connection and conversation are what builds trust.

- Politely but firmly end the interview with people who do not cooperate in the first five minutes. It's OK not to sell everyone.

- Never talk about yourself, your credentials or your company. Let people draw their conclusions about your competence and credibility by how you behave instead of by what you say. Have a simple brochure they can read at their leisure. Give it to them only if they ask.

- Insist prospects bring all their financial documents to the first meeting and expect them to cooperate.

- Begin asking where all the clients' money is, reviewing their financial documents and prioritizing their goals just 10–15 minutes into the first meeting.

- Let their own values and financial reality (Financial Road Map) motivate them to action. If their own truth doesn't move them emotionally, then they must not care more about their financial success than you do, so you should disengage. Using fear-based scare tactics and greed-oriented performance promises to sell financial products and services is a sign of poor skills or desperation, not the basis of a healthy and fruitful relationship.

- If you get objections, it's probably because you let someone slip through your filter who should have been shown the door in the first five minutes.
- Refuse to go to work for people without a commitment to do business with you.
- "Closing" is the natural outcome of conducting a good interview and creating an accurate financial strategy. *Once* is the correct number of times to ask them to take action.

Selling is not about closing; it is about opening: opening a high-trust relationship with people who want you to help them with their financial life more than you want to sell financial products.

That's a pretty big leap of faith. And I am asking you to make it. Go out into the real world, change what you have done in the past, embrace and implement the strategies of Values-Based Selling and see for yourself how well they work. The same good things will happen for you that happen for everyone who makes this transition. I have binders full of testimonial letters from people who have already made this change for the better. You are not a guinea pig. I would love to hear about your success with Values-Based Selling.

WHAT YOU CAN EXPECT WITH MASTERY OF VALUES-BASED SELLING

"I use your WIA ——— TY process in the initial discussion as you suggest. As many people have probably already told you, it works! It gets agreement and commitment a lot more quickly. I now charge fees, and your process helped me launch into that. I differentiate myself because nobody else asks my prospects and clients the questions you teach.

"I use their values in a follow-up letter after the initial interview, in the presentation as a reinforcement and in the discussion of my recommendations. Since I have been doing this, they don't have any objections because their core values, which I understand, lead them to do what they need to do for their own reasons."

—WILLIAM G. THARP II

The Key to Mastery of Values-Based Selling: Commitment

Just as you sometimes feel you care more about your clients' financial success than they do, one of my greatest frustrations is having people get very enthusiastic about the tools of Values-Based Selling but never translate their enthusiasm into action.

Real commitment means making a promise to yourself:

I will do whatever it takes, for however long it takes, until I get the results I want. It is impossible for me to fail because I use all feedback—good and bad—as information to help me become even better. You will see me standing proud at the end of my journey, or you will find me dead on the side of the road that leads there.

That is commitment.

I promise Values-Based Selling won't kill you. But if you work hard to master it, this approach *will* help you achieve greater financial independence, enjoy more time off, bridge the gap between where you are now and where you want to be and fulfill your own core values sooner than you might have without it. I didn't write this book so you could make a few more sales. I wrote it to help you make a quantum leap in your career while you create a simpler, more satisfying quality of life.

Mastering the Values-Based Client Interview

As with every new skill, mastering the values conversation takes practice and self-evaluation. It's been said that anything worth doing is worth doing badly—at least in the beginning. This doesn't mean you ever have to do the values-based interview badly; you may be really good at it from the beginning. But you must take the risk that you might not be as good at it when you first start as you will be after you practice and persist.

Think back to when you were learning to walk. Did you get up the first time you tried, stroll across the room with a little swagger, your baby arms swinging easily, and say, "Hey, Mom and Dad, look! I'm walkin'!" Probably not.

Learning to walk is one of our more challenging tasks as a toddler. It's a pretty remarkable feat, considering that crawling around doesn't work all that badly. Perhaps your current method of interviewing doesn't work that badly either. But if you want to learn how to stroll with the best in our business, you have to give up the old sales crawl and practice the values walk. If you apply the same determination to mastering Values-Based Selling as you did to walking, you'll be brilliant in a very short time. And the payoff is huge.

Following are five suggestions that will help you quickly learn the values-based interview and keep improving your skills even after you feel comfortable with it.

1. PRACTICE AND ROLE-PLAY THE INTERVIEW UNTIL YOU ARE VERY COMFORTABLE WITH ITS FLOW.

Record your practice on video- or audiotape. Then study the tape objectively to see what you can learn from it.

A brilliant client interview is a repetitive motion process much like a golf swing. While the people you meet may not be predictable, each phase of the interview process and the way you move along to the next phase are completely predictable. The greatest golfer cannot control exactly how her ball will land on the turf, but she does control how she swings the club to move it from where it is now to where she wants it to be. You will create the ideal flow for the interview by developing the ability to move people from one phase to the next. The values-based interview provides the structure, no matter how the client responds. The questions determine the flow, and the answers personalize the interview for that client.

Values-Based
Client Interview Model

First 5–10 Minutes

OBJECTIVE: Determine whether the prospect is *in* or *out*.
ACTION: Conduct the values conversation.
(The prospect is *in* if you've gained trust/cooperation and a positive emotional bond.)
Who should be talking? THEM!
ACTION *(In)*: Proceed to next 30–45 minutes.
ACTION *(Out)*: Politely disengage.

Next 30–45 Minutes

Candid discussion about the present	Candid discussion about the future as they want it to be
OBJECTIVE: Truth	**OBJECTIVE: Vision**
• Assets	**ACTION:** Ask questions to determine what the prospect wants the future to be.
• Situation	
• Facts	"What are your goals and desires (tangible stuff)?"
• Problems	"What would you like life to be like?"
	"Which goals require money?"

Who should be talking? THEM!

Next 10–15 Minutes
Visually Plot Using Financial Road Map

OBJECTIVE: Create a compelling picture that will motivate them to do business with you now.
ACTION: Plot where they are now, the goals and the emotional payoff. The answers are plotted on the Financial Road Map providing a compelling snapshot of their life from which they can now make intelligent choices, allowing them to achieve their goals and fulfill their values.

Overall Objective: Get a commitment that clients want you to help them bridge the gap between where they are now and where they want to be so they can feel a greater sense of values fulfillment. Discuss the parameters of your relationship and how much you charge.

If at any point the prospect or client chooses not to move from one phase to the next, end the meeting. To continue the golf metaphor, there is a tee shot, fairway shot(s), approach shot(s), chipping and putting—in that order. You either play each stroke in the proper order or you pick up your ball and stop playing that hole. You don't putt on the tee or drive on the green. To conduct an effective interview, you must follow a specific order also.

Rarely will a client's financial situation be so complex that a values-based interview runs longer than 60 minutes. If it does, chances are that it was hijacked into some superficial, unimportant matters, and you lost control of the flow. Or you talked too much.

Remember: Two sincere, intelligent, reasonable people who are being honest with each other should be able to come to a conclusion in 60 minutes about whether or not they can do business together. Prospects should have made one of three decisions as they consider the truth on their Financial Road Map:

- Yes, we do want to do something about this, and we want your help.

- Yes, we do want to do something about this, and we don't want your help.

- No, we don't want to do anything about this.

The truth of the prospects' financial situation and the gap they are facing almost always produces a reaction. Even very financially successful people have gaps in their financial realities or have not fully considered the relationship between their financial choices and their values. In fact, the most financially successful are the ones who like this approach the best and are quickest to take action. Wanting your help when they get to this point is a natural conclusion for them. When you're the person who facilitates the clients' discovery of their own financial reality, and you do so in the context of their core values, they will almost always turn to you for direction and guidance. But if they cannot make a decision you cannot help them.

2. AUDIOTAPE EVERY CLIENT INTERVIEW AND *LISTEN* TO THE RECORDING.

If we never looked in the mirror, how would we know what we look like? You have to listen to yourself to know what you sound like with prospects and clients. This will accelerate your mastery of the interview process. The following stage setting will enhance your credibility with your prospect. It shows that you take every meeting seriously, and it provides a rationale for the presence of the tape recorder.

> ***VBFP.*** Everything we discuss today is confidential. In addition to taking good notes during our meeting, I will audiotape our conversation. I will listen to this tape a couple of times before our next meeting to be absolutely sure I understand exactly what you want and my recommendations are accurate.

It's like when you watch a movie
for a second time, you see things
you missed the first time.
This will help me create the
best strategy for you.

My job is to help you make
smart choices about your money.
What's important about money
to you?

There are three perspectives from which to
assess the interview when you listen to your
tape:

1. The way you wanted it to flow
2. The way you remember it flowing
3. The way it actually did flow

In addition to discovering information that
will help you do a better job for your client,
you will listen to the tape to learn the truth of
how well you managed the client interview.
Your objective is to get the actual interviews to
flow like you planned.

While you are listening to the tape, fill out
a written self-evaluation. Consider the ideal
interview flow you prepared, and complete the
following self-evaluation.

Self-Evaluation—
The Values-Based Interview

1. **How did the values conversation go?**
   ❑ Very well ❑ Pretty well ❑ Just OK ❑ Not too well

2. **Were the prospects emotionally involved?** ❑ Yes ❑ No

3. **How could I tell?**

_____

_____

4. **Did I get all the way to their highest core values?** ❑ Yes ❑ No

5. **Am I clear about the difference between their values and their goals?**
   ❑ Yes ❑ No

6. **What were three things that went well in this values-based interview?**

_____

_____

7. **What one thing could I do to improve the interview?**

_____

_____

8. **What one or two specific problems and challenges do I want to work on next time?**

_____

_____

9. **How can I be better prepared for the next interview?**

_____

10. **Who did most of the talking?**

_____

_____

11. **How many minutes did I talk?** _____

12. **How many minutes did the prospects talk?** _____

13. **Did I establish the prospects' financial goals?** ❑ Yes ❑ No

14. **Did the prospects bring all their financial documents?** ❑ Yes ❑ No

15. **Did I discover where all the prospects' money is?** ❑ Yes ❑ No

16. **Did I use the Financial Road Map to illustrate the gap between where the prospects are now and where they want to be?** ❑ Yes ❑ No

17. **Did I get commitment from the prospects to the process of creating a financial strategy?** (Or did I disengage if the prospects refused to make a commitment?) ❑ Yes ❑ No

18. **Did I set an appointment to present my recommended financial strategy?**
   ❑ Yes ❑ No

You might imagine that some prospects will be uncomfortable with the audiotaping. On the contrary, clients tend to be impressed that you are so thorough with the details. Everyone who tapes their interviews reports incredible results. And explaining it the way I described earlier will increase your credibility from the very beginning of the interview.

Don't be too hard on yourself when you listen to your tapes. The audiotape is a benchmark from which you improve. Remember that even a poor values-based interview is probably superior to a traditional client interview.

3. IF YOU GIVE SEMINARS OR GROUP PRESENTATIONS, VIDEOTAPE THEM.

As a speaker, you represent the financial services industry and its highest standards. When you look at the videotape, use the same evaluation questions to measure your effectiveness with Values-Based Selling in seminars. (The seminar application of Values-Based Selling is covered in detail in Appendix B.)

4. ASK SOME PEOPLE YOU RESPECT TO REVIEW YOUR TAPED INTERVIEWS AND GIVE YOU FEEDBACK.

Have them fill out the self-evaluation for you.

5. INVEST IN THE VALUES-BASED SELLING TAPE SYSTEM.

A great tool for mastering the values conversation is the Values-Based Selling tape system we offer. Information on how to purchase this video/audio/workbook package is in the back of this book.

Keep Improving—
Mastery Is a Journey.

Even people who have been quite successful implementing Values-Based Selling feel they never truly master it; they always look for ways to get better. Continue to tape and self-evaluate so you're always moving away from selling by accident and moving toward your next level of success.

Audiotape your strategy presentations and statement reviews also, so you can hear how well you present the strategy, ask for commitment, update your clients and get referrals.

Have you set a benchmark for yourself in conducting the client interview? In golf your benchmark is par: You attempt to lower your handicap to scratch golf. In any endeavor, a benchmark is crucial to measuring improvement. Students strive for a 4.0 grade-point average, people who are health conscious set ideal body fat percentages and so on. What is your interview/client relationship benchmark, and how are you measuring your progress?

Get Your Ego Out of the Way.

Make sure your ego does not impede your progress. In his book *Mastery*, George Leonard discusses 13 pitfalls along the master's journey. Pitfall number 10 is vanity. Leonard writes, "It's possible that one of the reasons you got on the path of mastery was to look good. But to learn something new of any significance, you have to be willing to look foolish. . . . If you're always thinking about appearances, you can never attain the state of concentration that's necessary for effective learning and top performance."

It's unlikely you will actually look foolish, but you must be *willing* to look foolish for the sake of your own growth.

As you review tapes of your interviews, remember that they represent helpful information about your skill level. Use them as an incentive to improve. If, on a scale of 1 to 10, you are a 3, you need to know that so you can take the steps necessary to become a 4, then a 5, then a 6 and so on. However, if you are a 3 and don't know it, you may not be motivated to improve and you'll be stuck at 3. Worse yet, you may be a 5 but think you're a 9. The truth is important.

Many financial professionals who audiotape themselves describe listening to their tapes as a little painful. But they all agree that listening to their tapes definitely improved their skills.

Here are a few of their comments:

- "I had no idea I talked so much."

- "Listening to the tape, I heard things that were clearly more important than I had acknowledged them to be during the interview."

- "I said things I didn't remember saying, and they said things I didn't remember them saying."

- "I was all over the map. One minute I was over here talking about one topic, the next minute I was over there talking about something else. There was very little continuity."

- "There was too much chitchat and small talk. I took way too long to get down to business."
- "That explanation of myself and my company seemed to put them to sleep."
- "Client interviews obviously don't have to take nearly as long as they have taken in the past."

When you are happy with the tapes of your client interviews, your results will be incredible.

HIGHER CONVERSION RATIO

"I have been using your Values-Based Selling process for about one year now. I have to tell you that my conversion ratio from appointments to clients has dramatically increased (more than a 50% improvement). My meetings are shorter, and I believe it helps get clients focused right from the beginning."

C. LINDLAY GARNER, CFP

Self-Mastery: Walking Your Talk

Another mastery objective of Values-Based Selling is to achieve your own financial goals and fulfill your own values as you help others do the same. If you cannot honestly say you are following the advice you are giving to others, and if you are not on the road to financial independence and fulfilling your own values, you cannot succeed at your highest possible level. Mastery involves not just *doing* but also *being*. Self-mastery—being a "walk-your-talk" financial professional—is the ultimate trust builder.

As a VBFP, you are walking your talk when you have the following:

- A written personal financial strategy
- An objective financial professional (other than yourself) helping you implement your Financial Road Map
- The appropriate amount of insurance(s)
- Qualified retirement plans to which you make regular contributions
- Additional savings beyond the qualified plans (if this is required for your goals)
- Liquid cash reserves for emergencies
- Zero debt or a debt elimination strategy
- Increasing annual income coupled with decreasing work hours
- Regular coaching on your professional skills

VBFPs "walk their talk."

Follow the same proven principles for financial success that you advise your clients to follow: Create a financial strategy with a long-term perspective and live by that strategy, pay yourself first, subordinate short-term emotional gratification to long-term financial goals and value fulfillment, live within your means, believe in the truth of "what goes around comes around" and give generously.

Walking your talk is the ultimate trust builder. It's more than something you do. It is who you *are*. The more successful you become, the more you realize that people do not do business with you for what you do. They do business with you because of who you are. *Who are you?*

You demonstrate who you are by exemplifying the principles of a financially successful life. Although the principles are simple, living by them often isn't. The closer you come to doing for yourself what you advise others to do, the easier it is to influence your clients. There is an unspoken attraction to people who walk their talk.

Summary

- In every activity, the best results come from mastery.
- To master the values-based client interview, follow these guidelines:
  - ✔ Practice and role-play the prospect or client interview so you are very comfortable with its flow. Videotape or audiotape your practice.

- ✔ Audiotape every interview, listen to the recording, evaluate the strengths and weaknesses and improve.

- ✔ If you give seminars or group presentations, videotape those sessions, watch them, evaluate their effectiveness and improve.

- ✔ Ask someone you respect to listen to your audiotapes or watch your videotapes and give you feedback.

- You will know you are on the road to mastery when

  - ✔ you keep improving and looking for new ways to improve;

  - ✔ your ego doesn't impede your progress;

  - ✔ you "walk your talk."

EXERCISE

For your next prospect interview, use the values conversation and (with the prospect's knowledge) audiotape the interview. Listen to the audiotape and use a copy of the Self-Evaluation in this chapter to estimate the effectiveness of the interview. Decide how to improve for the next prospect interview. Write a reminder note to look at just before your next values conversation (e.g., *Talk less, listen more* or *Don't change the question*).

If you still feel more comfortable with your old interview techniques, audiotape one of those interviews. Use the same Self-Evaluation and compare the effectiveness of your old interview with the effectiveness of the values conversation for achieving commitment and total financial discovery.

Continue audiotaping and evaluating your values conversations. Decide specifically what to do to improve. Write it down, and congratulate yourself when you do it!

NOTES

Conclusion—
The Big Payoff

I love what I do for a living and I'll bet you do, too. However, there is much more to my life than being a speaker, author, consultant and coach. And I'll bet there is much more to your life than being a financial professional. What you may not have realized yet is that the more you expand who you are as a person, the more success you will have as a financial professional—no matter how successful you are now. Do all the dimensions of your life get the time they deserve? Are you having enough fun? Do you feel fulfilled and satisfied? Do you have a secret wish list of things you "someday" want to do or become?

No matter how much you love what you do for a living, if you want to lead a balanced life, you must make a lot of money—*and* take a lot of time off—to experience more of what life offers. **I believe an important aspect of leading a fulfilled life is to want for nothing financially without being a slave to making money.**

> ## "Never confuse having a career with having a life."
> EDDIE BAUER (ADVERTISEMENT)

Consider all the incredible things you might do if you only had the time and the money. Break free of those rigid inhibitions about what you "should" do or what you "can't" do. Let go of a work ethic that causes you to feel guilty when you take time off. Your life away from work is the payoff for becoming not merely a good but a *brilliant* financial professional.

It is my belief that the world was created for us to enjoy. You can be a caring, helping human being and have an incredible amount of fun, too. So take your time reading this chapter and begin dreaming. **If you had the next five years off with all expenses paid, and you could do anything but work, what would you do?**

Have you ever wondered what it would be like to attend every major sporting event in the world in a single year? The Super Bowl, the World Series, all four Grand Slam tennis tournaments, the Majors in golf, the Indy 500, the NBA Championships, the Final Four, the Stanley Cup, the Olympics, the Hawaii Ironman, the Boston Marathon, World Cup skiing, World Cup soccer, the Tour de France, the Heavyweight Boxing Championships, the Pipeline Masters surfing contest, the America's Cup or Whitbred races and all the other events you care about? Wow, what a year!

Maybe you'd rather participate. You can play the most famous golf courses in the world: Sawgrass, Inverness, Pebble Beach, the Old Course at St. Andrews, Augusta National, Baltusrol, Pinehurst National, Shinnecock Hills, Oakmont Country Club, Muirfield Village Golf Club, the Princeville course in Kauai and Oak Hill Country Club.

How good could your golf or tennis game become with the right amount of playing time and coaching? You can ski the most spectacular slopes in the world every winter and ski New Zealand in August if you want to. Or perhaps you want to create your own "endless summer" of surfing. Maybe you want to attend a fantasy sports camp.

Would you like to fish the best rivers, lakes or oceans at the perfect times of year? The fly-fishing for cutthroats, rainbows and brownies in Montana defies description, and the Marlin fishing off the coast of Cabo San Lucas is some of the best in the world.

Maybe you're starting to think, What about earning a living? **Of course you need money. But why take the whole year to earn it?** Who says you can only have two weeks, four weeks or six weeks of vacation?

Financial health. Physical health. Spiritual health. Relationship health. Mental health. These are the components of the truly balanced life, and to create optimum health in all these areas, you need to give them time and attention. *This* is what your time off is for.

How great could your marriage be? It is possible to truly understand your kids and have them *want* to be around you. How close would you like to be to your parents, your brothers and sisters and your best friends? It's nice to have the choice to home-school your children or send them elsewhere for a better education.

What would life be like if someone else ran all the errands, cleaned the house, did the laundry, mowed the lawn, washed the car, bought the groceries and cleaned out the garage? Not because you're lazy, but because your time is better spent with the people you care about, doing more important things together. Ben Franklin said, "A life of leisure and a life of laziness are not the same thing."

I'll bet there is an instrument you have always wanted to learn to play or play better— the piano, the drums, the guitar, the saxophone. If not now, when?

What charity do you want to donate more time or money to? No doubt, there is a church or synagogue that would benefit from more of your involvement.

Do you want to go whitewater rafting, rock climbing, bungee jumping, skydiving, surfing, kayaking, scuba diving, extreme skiing or snowboarding? You might do these things already, but maybe not nearly often enough.

How physically fit could you become? Could you run a 10k or a marathon, cycle a century or finish a triathlon? How about the Ironman? With the right weight training you could be buffed out. Or maybe you are ready just to start walking around the block, losing a few pounds or climbing a flight of stairs without breathing hard.

Do you want to fly a plane, a helicopter, a hang glider or an ultralight?

Where do you want to go? What do you want to do? Who do you want to become?

Here's how Charles Kuralt described the inspiration for his book, *Charles Kuralt's America*:

> *I planned a trip. I had spent nearly all my life traveling in the United States, but there was one more fanciful journey I had always wanted to make. Now I had the chance, and the prospect thrilled me: I would revisit my favorite American places at just the right time of year— the Florida Keys before it got too hot, the Minnesota canoe country before it got too cold, Charleston in azalea season, Montana in fishing season, Vermont when the oaks and maples turn crimson and gold. I would go to New Orleans and Alaska and the Blue Ridge Mountains and old New Mexico and the coast of Maine. I would go alone and without a plan and without a budget—I'd saved enough to live on for a while—and I wouldn't do anything*

that felt very much like work. I had never been any good at doing nothing; I thought I would try to learn.

I would drift with the current of life. I'd be footloose and a little irresponsible, and I'd have a perfect year in America.

Later in the book, Kuralt wrote about his experience off the coast of Maine while sailing with friends who had twice sailed around the world.

I suffered a pang of envy. I learned to sail when I was still young enough to cross an ocean and promised myself I'd do that someday at the helm of my own boat. **But promises postponed have a way of getting broken.** *Now I was too old, and my ability too rusty, and that particular dream, like so many others, was on the shelf for good.*

I wonder how many people who wait until they are retired to really start living feel, as Charles Kuralt does about sailing, "too old or too rusty." But they couldn't do it sooner because they were "too busy sacrificing themselves for the children." What better gift could you give your children than to demonstrate what it's like to really live? Do we want kids growing up today to think children are a burden to be sacrificed for? It's one thing if you really have to sacrifice. But you don't. You are a financial professional. *Your income and free time are totally within your control.*

Do you want to see the Taj Mahal, the Eiffel Tower, Big Ben, a bullfight, the Egyptian or Mayan pyramids, the Nile, rainforest, the Panama Canal, Glacier Bay, the South Pole, the Great Wall, the Great Barrier Reef? How would you like to drive cattle in Wyoming? (Yee ha!) You could spend a month in the Caribbean or the South Pacific, or go on an African safari, or trek over the Himalayas or watch whales migrate.

How come you speak only one language?

Maybe it's time to earn that black belt you have always wanted in the martial arts.

I've heard those race-car driving schools are a blast.

What would you study that has nothing to do with making money?

What about community service or running for political office? Take in a foreign exchange student. Volunteer to work with the disabled or the terminally ill.

At this writing, you can fly around the world on the Concorde for about $95,000 per couple. It takes 30 days and it's first-class everything. (This is not only a once-in-a-lifetime trip, it could be the best prospecting you ever experience!)

What would it be like to watch those crazy guys surf 30-foot waves in Waimea Bay on the North Shore of Oahu, or to catch the tulips blooming in Holland or to see the swallows return to Capistrano? *Promises postponed have a way of getting broken.* Plans never made have a way of never being carried out.

Maybe you want to learn to program your VCR, or surf the Internet or get good enough to beat your kids or grandkids at video games. Perhaps you'd just like time off at home to do nothing, watch old movies or finish off those incomplete projects.

Do you want to check into a nice spa to be "fluffed and buffed" or to hang out by the resort pool while they bring you bottomless Mai Tais?

You could become a consummate chef or a wine connoisseur.

How long would it take to visit all the wineries in the world?

How many unread books are on your shelves?

These ideas should jump-start your thinking. Maybe you work the whole year because you don't have enough reasons to become skilled enough to produce your results in much less time. With all there is to do in this world and all we are capable of being, it's remarkable that some people are unsure what to do when they're not working. How's *your* wish list coming along so far?

Ask for the moon . . . Shoot for the stars!

My Wish List

Take the Long View.

Let's get real for a moment: You are going to die. This is not a scare tactic, just a fact. It's probably going to happen sooner than anybody would like. At some point before then, you will look back on your life and wonder how and why it went by so quickly. You will wish you had done some things less, some things better, some things sooner, some things not at all and some things more.

When you are 80 or 90 or 100 years old, you will quite likely look back on your career and shake your head in amazement that you were ever afraid to

- ask for referrals;
- confront your clients and prospects about making the best financial choices;
- insist that your clients tell you where all their money is before you go to work for them;
- require your clients to bring all their financial documents to the first meeting;
- hone your skills to brilliance;
- listen to yourself on audiotape.

You may also look back on your life and wonder why you didn't

- take more risks,
- take more time off,
- tell people you loved them more often.

In 1994, *USA Today* cited a study of men's feelings as they grew older. The researchers asked men over 65 which they regretted more: things they did that hadn't worked out or things they never tried. You probably won't be surprised to learn that their response was 4:1 regretting what they *didn't* do. Looking back, they realized their reasons for not trying were foolish. The actual risks were far smaller than they had appeared to be at the time.

I'm sure you've heard that nobody on a deathbed has ever said, "I wish I had spent more time at the office." So spend less time working because you've gotten so good that you work less and produce more. When you are working, *produce results*. If you are not doing what produces results, *don't work*. **Put yourself in the position where you want for nothing financially, but are not a slave to making money.**

No Excuses

I have met a handful of very "successful" people in this business who have confided in me that they are miserable, even though they are top producers in their firms. One gentleman described for me the feelings of fraud he has every year when his company props him up at the national convention to give his speech about his success. He has been in the business more than 20 years, consistently earns more than $600,000 personal annual income, and would love to tell his colleagues *not* to be like him. He can't remember the last day he took off without calling the office. He has a couple of marriages behind him. He's missed important events his kids were involved in. And he's not in very good physical condition. I'll bet you know people like this at your company. They exist, whether you know them or not.

Unfortunately, some people use the unhappy workaholic as an excuse for their own choice to be mediocre. They claim, "I could be as successful as so-and-so, but I'm not willing to work that many hours because I want to be with my family." As if the only way to be successful is to be a workaholic. Someone should tell them, "If your family is so important, why don't you figure out how to make enough money by working a lot fewer hours so you can spend more quality time with these important people without sacrificing your quality of life?" It's too bad that some people choose to use what could be their greatest inspiration as their excuse for poor performance. And there are dozens of other excuses: the company, the manager, the home office, the government, taxes, the economy, interest rates, the markets, the state of the industry, public perception, the lousy staff, the biased media, my poor relatives and on and on.

None of this has anything to do with your choice to be at the top of your profession. *None.* In fact, **the more turbulent and unpredictable times are, the more attractive the most successful financial professionals become to the best clients.**

Hmmm . . .

Right now someone who is not as smart as you, who has less experience, in a worse market, with more personal problems, plus crummy credentials, and working for a low-rated company, is having a better year than you are. How come? Because he or she has *chosen* to.

Become brilliant at what you do. You know, this financial and insurance stuff ain't rocket science or brain surgery. No Ph.D. is required. (For that matter, no college degree is required.) The principles are quite simple. The process isn't complicated. This is a business you really can master. People who are the best at what they do are highly paid for the results they produce, not the hours they work. You don't work in a factory or in a coal mine. You don't farm the land. *That's* hard work. And it's not like you're an artist whose work will become valuable after you're dead. Your work is valuable now. So no more excuses. Just choose the quality of life you want, and produce it!

How Much Is Enough?

I am not suggesting, as Gordon Gekko in the film *Wall Street* did, that "Greed is good." I am encouraging you to figure out how much is enough *for you* and to become good enough to earn that much in substantially less than the whole year. Write down some tangible reasons to get this good, be clear about your own values, and the people you care about will be the only other fuel you need to create your successful, balanced life.

It is easy to underestimate how much money you need to generate to have the life you want. Be honest about *your* numbers and work them out for yourself. From your current gross income, can you

- pay off your debts,
- cover your current business expenses,

- save a business cash reserve,
- pay your taxes (on time),
- save and invest for financial independence (or retirement),
- save in advance for vacations, holiday gifts, and special events (like college),
- give 10% to church or charity,
- create an appropriate personal cash reserve,
- have adequate insurance,

. . . and still have enough *net, spendable income* left over to pay your personal expenses and live the quality of life you really want? If your answer is no, you might have to make more money or make some adjustments in what you do with your money. How much must you earn in order to live the principles you represent as a financial professional and lead the balanced life that will make you happy?

No-Nonsense Advice

"I say you ought to be rich; you have no right to be poor. You and I know that there are some things more valuable than money. . . . Nevertheless, the man of common sense also knows that there is not any one of those things that is not greatly enhanced by the use of money."

RUSSELL H. CONWELL
Acres of Diamonds

Become a Magnet.

I believe in the philosophy that you do not pursue success; rather, you *attract* success by the person you become. The more you become, the more you attract. The more you give, the more you get. Same principle. The more you study your craft of being a brilliant financial professional, the better you become. Therefore, you attract the clients you want, and you don't pursue them. Living a full life will make you a financial professional who attracts quality clients. The Million Dollar Round Table (MRDT) calls this the "whole person" concept. I like that. Give it a try.

I encourage you to read this chapter again later and use it to stimulate your thinking. Read it with your spouse or your entire family to create your own payoff list. I created this chapter from my own list of things to do and become. I also asked other people to answer this question: **If someone would replace your income to allow you to do anything you wanted for the next five years, except work, what would you do?** Remember, there is a relationship between your financial health, your physical health, your relationship health, your mental health and your spiritual well-being. Who must you become for your goals to be achieved and your values fulfilled? Become that person. Don't just be a financial professional; be a financial example. Be a quality of life example.

Smart Financial Choices
Impact the Quality of Your Life.

Mental Health

Spiritual Health

Financial Health

Relationship Health
Family • Friends
Clients • Colleagues

Physical Health

Summary

- As a financial professional, you can have it all: the money you want, the time off you want and the satisfaction of a successful career.
- Living the life you want to live, doing the things you want to do, pursuing the achievements you seek—all these make you a better, more interesting person and contribute to your financial, relationship, physical, mental and spiritual health.
- You attract success by the person you become.

EXERCISE

Look at your wish list. Are you on the right financial track to be able to achieve your dreams and fulfill your values?

1. If you haven't already incorporated Values-Based Selling into your business, start today. If you have one appointment with a prospect, a new client or an existing client, use the values conversation to start building a high-trust relationship.

2. If you have practiced the values conversation and you are trying to master it, don't give up. The life you want awaits you. If one or two sticky problems block the way to your mastery of Values-Based Selling, send me an e-mail (info@bachrachvbs.com) describing your concerns, and I will do what I can to help you with those roadblocks.

NOTES

APPENDIXES

More Paths
to Mastery

A. How to Conduct the Values Conversation With Couples

For any Values-Based Financial Professional (VBFP), the key to having the values conversation with couples is to engage only one person at a time. Start with one and work your way completely through the values conversation with him or her. Then switch and work with the second person.

How to Handle the Dominant Partner

In most relationships, one person tends to dominate. **Always work with the less dominant person first.** This helps the less dominant person answer the values questions independently and prevents echoing the more dominant person's answers.

How do we know who is less dominant? Sometimes your instinct will tell you. Body language clues and who seems to

take charge in the meeting can all help you detect immediately who is less dominant. If it's not immediately obvious, you can simply ask who wants to go first; the dominant person will invariably volunteer to go first.

The sample conversation below indicates what an effective values conversation sounds like with a married couple, Bob and Mary. In this example, imagine that you have determined by her body language and take-charge attitude that Mary is the dominant person, so you want to work with Bob first.

Notice how the VBFP's setting the stage . . .

VBFP. The first step to creating an intelligent financial strategy is to invest a few minutes in thinking about what's important. Most of what we do will be a collaboration. Our first exercise, however, requires input from each of you separately. We'll begin with you first, Bob. Then, Mary, you and I will discuss the same question. Bob, what's important about money *to you?*

At this point, you would fill in Bob's answers in the WIA ——— TY staircase. Complete the entire conversation with Bob, then proceed with Mary, starting again with, "What's important about money *to you?"*

Now suppose that as this couple settled in at your office, your instincts didn't really help clarify who was the dominant person. In that case, you can begin the conversation by asking who wants to start, then explaining that you will begin with the other partner. Here's how it sounds:

VBFP. The first thing we are going to do today calls for me to get each of your perspectives about a key issue that relates to the work we do. Who wants to go first?

Mary. I will.

VBFP. I have a funny little philosophy, Mary. I always work first with the person who doesn't volunteer. So, Bob, we'll begin with you today. Your turn will come in a few minutes, Mary. My job is to help you make smart choices about your money. Bob, what comes to mind when I ask, what's important about money *to you?*

Bob. Security.

Write Bob's answer in the bottom line of his WIA ——— TY staircase, and you're on your way. Work your way to the top; then have the values conversation with Mary.

Not all conversations with couples go so smoothly, of course. The dominant person will sometimes interrupt, either trying to lead or help. This is a great opportunity to establish that you are in charge of the interview. Remember again that you are a professional trying to make an accurate financial diagnosis; what do you think a doctor would do if the spouse kept interrupting and answering the questions the doctor needed to get from the patient?

Let's see how the conversation might work if the VBFP is engaged in the values conversation with Bob, but Mary interrupts.

VBFP.   Bob, what's important about money *to you?*

Mary.   Bob likes . . .

VBFP.   [*Immediately interrupting Mary before she can finish her comment.*] Now, Mary, this is Bob's turn. I promise we'll get to you in a few minutes. For most things, we will collaborate. But for this particular question, it is imperative that I get individual perspectives from each of you without any influence from the other. Is that OK with you?

Mary.   OK.

VBFP.   Back to you, Bob. What's important about money *to you?*

Always handle the interrupter in a lighthearted but firm manner. Yet be aware that, with dominant people, the first time is seldom the charm. What if Mary persists and interrupts again? Then you establish the ground rules again.

VBFP.   [*Smiling broadly.*] Mary, I thought we clarified the rules here. Bob goes first, and then it's your turn. This is your last warning. One more interruption, and I'm going to have to send you to the penalty box.

Mary.   [*Chuckling.*] OK. OK. I'm sorry. I won't interrupt again.

VBFP.   I'll tell you what. How about if
I give you a sheet of paper and
a pen so you can write your
answers down while Bob and
I have our conversation?

Mary.   OK.

The Myth of the Decision Maker

Certain old-school sales doctrines taught us
to focus on the more dominant person because
he or she would be the person who'd make the
ultimate decision. This philosophy does not
apply today in the financial services business.
Although one person may influence the
decisions more than the other, the less
dominant person often has veto power. Follow
this conversation between Bob and Mary on the
drive home after a meeting during which the
VBFP keyed in on Mary as the decision maker.

Mary.   That was great! I'm really excited
about getting started with our
financial planning and investing
for our future. It's about time we
took charge.

Bob.   I agree. But I'm not sure this is
the right person for us to work
with. I can't put my finger on
why, but I just don't have a good
feeling about this guy. I don't
think I trust him enough to be
the person to guide us through
our financial decisions.

At this point, it's over. Although this discussion may continue for a few more minutes, it is highly unlikely that Mary will be able to overcome Bob's feelings that he doesn't trust the financial professional. They will probably meet with someone else and end up working with an individual they *both* feel good about.

The Values Advantage With Couples

You already know that the values conversation with individuals gains their trust and helps them understand themselves better. The power of the conversation can be even stronger with couples. As each person listens to the other talk about values, one may discover new things about the other.

After you have conducted the values conversation with each person, you may need to let the two people talk to each other for a few minutes about the surprises or differences in their values. This will probably be an honest exchange at a deep emotional level. Being included in this type of exchange is a positive sign to you: The couple is working toward deciding the values that will motivate them to take your advice and, in the process, they are learning more about each other while you are learning more about them.

B. How to Use the Values Conversation With Groups and in Seminars

Throughout this book, I have presented Values-Based Selling as if you were talking and working with only one or two people at a time. But the Values-Based Financial Professional (VBFP) often works with multiple decision makers (such as boards of directors or pension groups) and sometimes conducts financial seminars for groups. Some companies will "interview" several financial professionals by having them make presentations during a meeting. It may be difficult to understand how the values conversation can fit into this setting; however, not only does it fit in, but it provides you with a sharp competitive edge over the other presenters the board may see.

When you are asked to present before multiple decision makers, use the following guidelines to help them decide on you in advance.

Before the Meeting

Before the meeting, first call the contact person for the group and say something like, "You know, one thing I'm sure your decision makers hate is when people give general presentations that don't specifically address their concerns. With that in mind, I'd like to call each of them and ask to talk with them for ten minutes so that I can tailor my presentation exactly to your situation." Personally, I've never had anyone refuse me, because my contacts always agree with the premise: Everybody hates generic presentations.

Call each of the decision makers and start a conversation like the following.

VBFP. As you know, next Tuesday at 10 o'clock, I'm going to be one of several people presenting how my company might help you with financial management. I've made enough of these presentations to know that you hate it when people make a generic presentation and understand neither your business nor your specific situation. So, if you can give me just five or ten minutes, it will help me tailor my presentation.

After the decision maker agrees, conduct the values conversation to learn about goals and current concerns.

It's very important to go through this process with each of the decision makers so you develop a bond with all of them. They will be impressed with your presentation, so unless you're really bad at it you already have an advantage.

During the Presentation

Whenever you conduct the values conversation to prepare for a presentation to a group, remember that the client is yours to lose. The decision makers are familiar with you; they don't even know your competitors. Your phone conversations before the meeting allow you to be on more familiar terms with the board members than any of your competitors, who may not even know the names of the decision makers.

There are two powerful ways to use your advance work during the presentation. First, thank the decision makers for helping you personalize your presentation. That impresses upon them that you took the time to call each of them and acknowledges their help. It also can send your competitors into a panic because none of them have that familiarity—especially if you are presenting last, your competitors realize that they're done, it's over and they can't recover from your advantage over them.

Second, weave throughout your presentation how your company's features and benefits apply to their specific situation, as they've discussed it with you. In your presentation, use their core values to enhance the feelings of trust, to continue to build your credibility and to

A Sterling Example

A participant at one of my seminars was a pension specialist who asked how the values conversation works with groups, so I explained it to him: Call all the decision makers, find out their values, acknowledge their help, and weave their values into your presentation.

He tried this approach for his next presentation to a pension group only a few days later. To make a long story short, not only was he entrusted with managing the $4 million 401(k) account, but he also became the personal financial professional for the chairman of the board. This all happened literally days after he first learned about using the values conversation. If you need more proof than that, find yourself a group and try the technique yourself. If you follow my guidelines specifically as I have described them, this technique will work amazingly well for you, too.

stimulate the emotions that create buying momentum.

Using Values in Seminars

The purpose of this section is not to sell the idea of giving a financial seminar or to teach the best way to give seminars. I simply want to tell you, if you are already giving seminars, it is still important to build a bond of trust in the first few minutes of the presentation—just as important as it is to build trust with an individual prospect. Also, I want to show by dialogue the way to integrate values into your seminars and to give a few tips that will generally enhance what you already do when you present a seminar.

Besides being your single most powerful tool in face-to-face meetings, the values conversation works great with large groups of people. It sets the tone effectively with your seminar audience and gets them to participate immediately. This quickly starts building high-trust relationships and creates buying momentum.

I built my whole business doing seminars about money. I love seminar marketing! It's a great way to get your message across to lots of qualified prospects and set appointments at the same time. Remember, the goal of the seminar is to build trust and set appointments.

Beginning the Values-Based Presentation

At the beginning of your presentation, draw a large green dollar sign at the bottom of the page of a flip chart. Open your presentation by acknowledging something like the following:

> **VBFP.** On a Tuesday evening in La Jolla, there are a lot of other things you could be doing besides attending a financial seminar. So, I know that you wouldn't have come here tonight if you weren't serious about making smart choices about your money.
>
> I don't know about you, but I always hate it when I go to a seminar, and the person giving the seminar doesn't seem to understand anything about me as a person and just gives the same old canned seminar. So, let me get your perspective on a very important question: What's important about money *to you?*
>
> [*Taking the caps off all the markers and holding a handful of markers ready to write answers on the flip chart.*]

This activity gives the audience members a little time to collect their thoughts and their courage enough to speak out. When no one responds by the time all the caps are off all the markers, gently encourage participation.

VBFP. Did anyone tell you this would be a participatory seminar? I need your responses to this. You don't have to raise your hands—just shout them out! What's important about money *to you?*

Stand there holding the markers until somebody says something. As the audience starts responding, randomly write down the answers on the flip chart. If someone says "security," print *security* somewhere on the page, perhaps at an angle. Then say, "What else? What's important about money *to you?*" Get 10 to 12 responses, and print each randomly, in different colors, across the flip chart. (Have plenty of bright markers for use on the flip chart. Mr. Sketch Markers write nicely and have a wide variety of colors.) Use appealing, bright, rainbow colors like blue, purple, red, fuchsia and green. Print the values large enough so that the whole audience can read them.

Sometimes an audience member will shout out something that is a goal, like sending a child to college, rather than a value. Here's how to reply: "Yes, that's something you want to *do* with your money. What's important about sending your child to college to you?" Or, I suggest you have two flip charts, one for their values and one for their goals. That way, nobody's answer is "wrong." You can reply to a goal by saying something like, "Great. That's a goal. That's something you do with your money." Write *college* on the goals flip chart, then quickly move back to the values chart and repeat the main question: "What's important about money *to you?*" And if somebody speaks up with "retirement," walk back to that goals chart and write it down. Everybody gets positive reinforcement, but you always turn them back to the values question: "Yes, retirement is something else you want to *do* with your money. You want to have enough money to retire. What's important about having enough money to retire and do all the things you want *to you?* What's important about money *to you?*"

Your values chart will be filled with the same types of responses you receive when you deal with individuals: freedom, accomplishment, making a difference, security, financial independence, spiritual fulfillment, self-esteem, etc.

Leave that page as it is, so that during the entire seminar, these emotional words written in these bright colors—the values—will be constantly in front of the audience. For the person for whom security is a high core value, "security" stands out throughout the presentation; "peace of mind" stands out to the person for whom it is a high core value, and so on.

After your values chart is full, go back to the goals chart and say, "You've already given me a couple of examples of what you want to *do* with your money. Sending children to college, retirement. What else do you want to *do* with your money? What are some other *goals?*" Put the goals in a linear, not random, list.

Next, be sure to "sell" the seminar. In other words, help your audience to know in advance what to expect and when to feel that they've received value.

VBFP. We've got a short period of time together. We're only going to spend 45 minutes here tonight, and I'm sure you came here to get some practical ideas that will get results. So, let me ask you a question: Suppose, at the end of the 45 minutes, you could walk through those doors saying, "Yes, I got something here that will really help me make smart financial choices about my money, so that I can not only achieve all my financial goals, but I can also [*naming values listed on flip chart*] have security, make a difference in peoples' lives and have a sense of accomplishment." Suppose, by the time we're done, you have heard real ideas that will help you achieve your goals and get what's important *to you*. Would you say then that this has been a good investment of your time?

Sounds a lot like precommitment, doesn't it?

Usually you'll get a verbal response. However, if it's a quiet group, just nod your head and say jokingly, "That's okay. Head signals will be fine, in which case this [*nodding head up and down*] will be yes and this [*shaking head from side-to-side*] will be no. I can work with that." Your audience needs to see very quickly that you're comfortable and quick on your feet, that you want to involve them, and that you will listen to what they say.

311

To arouse their curiosity, finish selling the seminar this way: "If you are really going to get value here, two things must happen. The first is being here tonight. I'll share the second with you later."

During the Presentation

It doesn't matter what the main subject of the seminar is. For any subject relating to money, you can and must weave in the values that your audience has shared with you. For example, if you are explaining the effectiveness of a living trust, you can say, "Putting together a living trust is a very smart financial decision because it allows you to maximize the marital exclusion. This is a smart choice about your money and might also help you have a greater sense of security and freedom [*and any other applicable values that this group has mentioned*]. It will clearly help those of you who have a goal of passing on the largest amount of money to your heirs [*and any other applicable goals the group has mentioned*]."

This may sound like something you would have said in any case. But this audience doesn't know this. The audience assumes that you are carefully considering their specific values and goals they have mentioned and that you are reacting to their input in order to personalize the seminar for them.

Whatever specific kind of seminar you're giving, it all comes back to money. For example, suppose you are giving an estate-planning seminar. You can start out by saying, "On a

Tuesday evening in La Jolla, there are a lot of other things you could be doing besides attending an estate-planning seminar. I know you wouldn't have come here tonight if you weren't serious about making smart choices about money, because estate planning is all about money. So, let me get your perspective on a very important question: What's important about money *to you?"*

At every opportunity, draw attention back to their values and show how your products and services help them fulfill their values. That makes the presentation totally personalized.

Setting Appointments at the Seminar

A big time waster for many seminar presenters is following up to make appointments that could easily have been set right after the seminar. Throw out those stupid forms that say, "If you'd like to have a free consultation, check this box." If they want the free consultation, they can set an appointment as they leave the seminar.

Make it really convenient for them to set the appointment. Place at least two six-foot tables at either side of the door(s) for appointment setting as participants leave the seminar. For every ten "buying units," you need two people available to set appointments after you conclude your meeting. Have an equal number of males and females; select people who look professional and can think and converse clearly. Provide each of these people with an appointment book.

Close your seminar by asking for commitment.

> **VBFP.** By a show of hands, how many of you feel the information you received and the time we shared today was a good use of your time and will help you make smart choices about your money?

Now, take a marker and hold it out with your arm stretched toward someone in the front.

> **VBFP.** Now, the second thing that has to happen for you to get value from this program is to find out how this will work for *you*. So, please, come on up here and write down for all of us some financial information. We just need your income, net worth, tax bracket, where your money is invested, etc.

Wait a few seconds for the collective anxiety to set in. Expect the person to look at you like you're crazy, like there's no way in the world he or she will reveal personal financial details in front of this group. (The person may even say, "I don't want to do that.")

Reassure the participant (and the audience).

> **VBFP.** Of course, I wouldn't really expect you to do that. Your personal financial information is exactly that—personal. But the problem is that now you've got some general information that can be applied to many people's financial situa-

tions—and you haven't had a chance to discover how that information applies to your personal financial situation. Because we know you need to know how all this works for you personally, we offer each of you an individual, private consultation. We will look at your personal financial situation confidentially so you can determine how the information you've heard here can benefit you personally. Otherwise, the time we've spent together is wasted. The first consultation is free.

I know what you're thinking: There's no such thing as a free . . .

[*Pausing to allow the audience to fill in the word* lunch *to keep them participating.*] We meet with you for two reasons. First, it's the right thing to do. It would be unprofessional to give this seminar and not help you discover how it works for you personally. Second, this is how we market our services. Let me put all of our cards on the table. We will meet with all of you. Half of you will need our services, become clients and think we're wonderful. The other half will get value from our time together, not need to become clients and you, too, will think we're wonderful. We don't know which half is which. What we do know is that it's good business for all of you to think we're wonderful. So take us up on our offer and find out exactly how what we discussed this evening applies to your personal situation.

This statement takes the pressure off, because most participants expect they will be the ones who do not need your help.

VBFP. So the next step is this. On your way out of this room, make an appointment for an individual consultation.

[*Turning and waving.*] If you look to the back of the room now, you'll see my assistants who are ready to set appointments with you on your way out. As you can see, they appear to be very nice people.

[*Smiling.*] However, I can't be held responsible for what might happen if you were to try to get past them without setting your appointment.

Your audience will laugh as they set appointments on their way out.

Don't worry about appointment overlap. If two appointments do overlap, you will call one of the prospects and reschedule the appointment.

Have your assistants give each prospect a list of financial documents the prospects must bring to the one-on-one meeting plus the written-in date and time of that meeting.

You'll find that the individual appointments go very smoothly because the seminar participants have already gone through the stage setting (they know why you are asking these questions), they have started to think about their own core values and perhaps have even written them down, they have mentally made a precommitment because they like your style and your methods and they are ready to quickly transition into full discovery during the first appointment.

Done effectively, this process will bring you a 90% or greater buying-unit-to-appointment closing ratio. Up to 100% is not uncommon.

INCREASE YOUR RATIO!

"My buying unit–to–appointment ratio at my seminars was consistently 90%. I never thought I could achieve a 100% appointment ratio, but that's exactly what happened the first time I applied what you teach."

HOWARD KALOOGIAN
Estate Planning Attorney

PERSONALIZE PRESENTATIONS WITH THE VALUES QUESTION.

"Normally, with a trusting group, my participation was always good (75-80%, with about 30% asking for a full planning session or help with CDs, IRAs, LI, etc.). When all was said and done at this meeting, we had a whopping 93% participation, and 71% of those asked to do additional business with us. The only change was the values question."

LIZ GIRARD
Personal Consulting Associates

Tips for Effective Values-Based Seminars

The following tips may help you in preparing and presenting any seminar, but the focus here is how to add credibility to the values-based approach.

- Ask someone to introduce you—someone who is good at introductions and will help you start out with credibility. You can write the introduction yourself and ask a colleague to present it.

- More light equals more energy. Low light equals low energy. Make sure the room is brightly lit throughout the entire presentation. Unless you have rear projection, a professionally lit stage and lights over the audience, never ever use slides again—because you can't use slides in a fully lit room.

  The subject of this book is building trust. Are you going to build trust when you're talking from the shadows? If you're a voice from the dark, you're

probably not building trust. You want them to see you and to see you are smiling and sincere. You want to give them an hour of well-lit, genuine caring.

If you need visuals for your presentation, give the participants a workbook so that they have their own sets of visuals or use overhead transparencies that are visible in a well-lit room. Place the projector and the screen in one corner that you can darken if needed without darkening the whole room. The transparencies should be full color, with very little writing on each one. *Do not read them to your audience.*

Set your room up classroom style so the participants can easily take notes. Make sure each participant has a pencil and notepad. Conduct your seminar like a workshop, a learning experience.

- Never "overseat" the room by putting out more seats than the number of participants you expect.

- Have water available so participants won't need to leave the room if they get thirsty. It also provides a means of interaction among the participants, as they pass the water pitcher to one another.

- Use a microphone. Even if your group is as small as 25, it looks professional to use a microphone, and if your audience is older, they will very much appreciate the amplified sound.

C. How to Handle Resistance When Resetting the Stage

Over the years, I have found that prospects find unique ways to avoid answering Values-Based Financial Professional's (VBFP's) WIA ——— TY questions. The following are examples of resistance that I have encountered and how I dealt with each kind of resistance.

Special Note: I am not recommending you memorize any of these responses. The resistance you receive may come in different forms, and your own personality will dictate the phrasing of your resetting the stage. Just notice the common threads in these examples.

1. Empathize or agree with the prospect.

2. Explain briefly that you are the professional and you know best how to go through the process.

3. Ask the WIA ——— TY question again. If you do not get cooperation after two resettings, politely disengage. This prospect will not be a Great Client.

"Don't Ask Me Questions."

Prospect. [*Wanting to find out about* only *retirement planning, mutual funds, estate taxes, or some other single area.*] I really don't want to answer any questions.

I just want to find out about retirement.

VBFP. I understand completely. The common denominator for retirement is money. It would be unprofessional for me to begin to recommend specific solutions for your needs until I understand what's important about money to you. I promise I will help you make smart decisions so you can achieve your primary goal. Help me understand: What's important about money *to you?*

"Who Are You?"

Prospect. Tell me about your company and your credentials.

VBFP. I'd be happy to. The best way to discover what I do and how it is done is to begin to *experience* it for yourself. Because you and I have limited time together, I have reserved this time for us to actually accomplish something of value for you. This is the best way for you to determine if I am qualified and if my company is any good. The written explanation of who I am, the strength and security of my company and my credentials can all be found in this brochure. After our meeting today, I invite you to read it thoroughly. Since

what I do is help people make
smart choices about their money,
the most professional thing for
me to do is to find out your perspective about the importance
of money. Help me understand:
What's important about money
to you?

"Tell Me How It Works."

Prospect. I don't want to answer any questions. I came here today to find
out what you do and how it
works.

VBFP. I understand completely. The best
way to find out what I do and
how it works is to *experience* it for
yourself. It takes less time to do it
than it does to explain it. Since
financial strategizing is about
money, the first thing a competent financial professional does is
to clarify what's important about
money *to you.* What's important
about money *to you?*

OR

VBFP. I understand. I want to help you
get what you want. It actually
takes longer to explain the
process than to walk through the
process. I recognize that this is
new for you; however, I do this
all the time. That's why people
like you work with people like

323

me. *There is a process and it works.*
By the end of our time together,
you will not only have a clear
understanding of what I do and
how it works, you will understand
specifically how it works for you.
The first step to the process of
enjoying a successful financial life
is to be clear about the importance
of money to you. Help me understand: What's important about
money *to you?*

"Prove That You Are Competent."

Prospect. How do we know that you are
competent or if we should follow
your advice?

VBFP. You don't yet. The only real way
to discover if I am competent or
not is to *experience* my competence. The process of making
smart financial choices is really
quite simple. If you are sincere
about making smart financial
choices I suggest you let me take
you through the process. Long
before it's time to give me any
money, you will know I am
competent. The first step to the
process of enjoying a successful
financial life is to be clear about
the importance of money to you.
Help me understand: What's
important about money *to you?*

"Just Give Me the Information."

Prospect. All I want is to learn about mutual funds. Can you just tell me what mutual funds are and how they work?

VBFP. I appreciate where you are coming from, but the answer is no, not with complete accuracy. Individual choices concerning mutual funds do not happen in a vacuum. Your entire financial situation affects every other financial choice you make, including mutual funds. For me to just sell you something to meet a need without understanding the dynamics of your entire financial life would be unprofessional. If I were to simply focus on this one thing without a comprehensive understanding of your situation, you would surely end up with a less than optimal solution. I'm only interested in the optimal, accurate solutions for my clients. It's your money; how about you?

Prospect. Yes, I suppose that makes sense.

VBFP. Good. In a few minutes, we may be discussing mutual funds and your other financial options. There is a method to my madness. First, we need to think about what's important about money to you. Help me understand: What's important about money *to you?*

"You Should Already Know That."

Prospect. It seems to me that you are the financial professional here. If you don't understand what's important about money, then maybe I'm in the wrong place!

VBFP. You're absolutely right. I understand what's important about money to me. And I understand what's important about money to all my other clients. However, it would be completely unprofessional for me to give you financial advice until I understand what's important about money *to you.* Help me understand: What's important about money *to you?*

"It's My Money."

Prospect. It's my money and I'll decide what we do in this meeting.

VBFP. You are right. It is your money. Ultimately every decision about what to do with it will be yours. However, it is my job to guide you through the most intelligent process for discovering your options so you can make the most intelligent decisions of what to do with your money. I understand that you are used to being in charge. But, here, when it comes to financial strategizing, I'm in charge of guiding you through the best process. If you have a better method than mine, then maybe you don't need my services. You obviously came here for a reason; instead of fighting my questions, why not just answer them? You just might find I'm quite good at what I do. What would you like to do?

"I Know What I Need."

Prospect. I think I have a pretty good idea of what we need to do.

VBFP. Terrific. You will probably find the framework we set up very easy to work through then. During our conversation, there will be plenty of opportunity to share your perspective. Much of what we do will probably reinforce your thinking. It's kind of like going to the doctor with a self-diagnosis. Only a quack would prescribe treatment purely on a patient's diagnosis. We have a very thorough process for making the smartest financial choices possible. More important than the products you buy are the people you choose to do business with. Unlike a visit to the doctor, this conversation isn't costing you anything. The first step to the process of enjoying a successful financial life is to be clear about the importance of money to you. Help me understand: What's important about money *to you?*

"You're Not Flexible."

Prospect. Your system doesn't seem very flexible.

VBFP. Thank you. The results and the specific solutions are extremely flexible and tailored just for you and your situation. However, you are absolutely right: the process isn't very flexible. It's not supposed to be flexible. It's supposed to produce results, and it does. Warren Buffet is worth billions. His strategy for selecting investments is not flexible. But boy, does it work! So sometimes inflexibility is comforting rather than a hindrance to effectiveness. Do you think Vince Lombardi was "flexible" with his players in mastering the fundamentals of football? Is the coach of an Olympic gymnastic team "flexible" in what it takes to win a gold medal? Of course not. Are your personal finances more or less important than a Super Bowl victory or gold medal?

Prospect. My personal finances are more important.

VBFP. Exactly. That's why my company and I have gone to great lengths to establish the ideal process for making the most intelligent financial choices. This will become obvious to you after you have experienced the process. The first step is to be clear about the importance of money *to you*. Help me understand: What's important about money *to you?*

"That's Weird."

Prospect. That's a weird question.

VBFP. You're right. It is a weird question. However, when you think about it, how can anyone help you make smart choices about your money until they understand what's important about money to you? At first, it may seem weird. But I assure you that it is essential. Help me understand: What's important about money *to you?*

D. How to Handle Reluctance to Provide Referrals

Giving referrals helps the client who gives them. If you don't believe that, your clients won't either.

I cannot overemphasize how important it is for you as a Values-Based Financial Professional (VBFP) to acknowledge the following truth and to change your business habits as a result of this truth: Every moment you are spending prospecting and marketing is a moment you are not investing in becoming a better financial professional. Ultimately, in order to achieve your highest level of success, you must be a brilliant financial professional, and it takes a certain amount of time and energy to develop into that type of financial professional. Prospecting and marketing do not make you a better financial professional. Every moment of prospecting and marketing takes you away from what you need to do to improve your skills, including the following:

- Reading and studying the best financial decision makers in history (the Warren Buffets of the world)
- Studying for your CFP, CLU, CHFC or other certificate programs that may enhance your understanding of how to be a better financial professional
- Taking courses on listening skills or the psychology of investors
- Working on interview skills to help prospects comfortably disclose all their financial assets
- Studying the psychology of your target market
- Calling your clients in a timely manner with ideas that will help them achieve their goals and fulfill their values
- Learning how to run your business so you can take more time off

When you master the client interview, you will never have to worry about new clients being reluctant to give you referrals. However, I want to give you some sample dialogues for two reasons:

1. To make you aware of ways to effectively handle people who at first hesitate to provide referrals
2. To motivate you to get so good at building trust in the client interview you rarely, if ever, have to use any of these dialogues

If you find yourself using these dialogues very often, you know either that you haven't built enough trust in earlier phases of the process or your clients are not all that impressed with your work. Pay attention to these signs. They are valuable coaching tools for your client development skills.

If something has occurred to make the client uncomfortable, it is important to discover it *immediately*. Otherwise, it may come up later in a way that could cost you the relationship.

> **VBFP.** You seem a bit reluctant to introduce me to people like you, who meet my profile. Do you feel the work I have done for you is valuable?
>
> **Client.** Of course.
>
> **VBFP.** I promise to handle your referrals professionally, just as you would expect me to. Have you been uncomfortable with anything that's happened in our relationship?
>
> **Client.** No.
>
> **VBFP.** We should treat the people you introduce me to as adults and let them make up their own minds. If my phone conversation with them reveals a good reason for them to get together with me, they will meet with me. There's no pressure; that choice will be theirs. Let's have another look at the profile and consider who among your colleagues or friends are always looking to make smart financial choices and improve their quality of life.

Sometimes clients do not understand immediately how giving you referrals benefits them. Restate the benefits to the client for giving you referrals.

VBFP. All of my clients expect a high quality of service from me. I imagine that you have high expectations, as well. Is that true?

Client. Of course.

VBFP. What I am trying to do is be completely honest with you about the reality of the financial services business. If I ever have to start advertising and cold prospecting, or implement expensive marketing techniques, it will affect you and my other clients in two ways: First, the time I spend cold prospecting is time that I can't spend focused on the financial events that affect my clients. I am a human being with only so many "units" of time. Wouldn't you like me to spend most of my time learning about ideas that could positively impact your financial life as well as helping you avoid situations that could negatively impact your financial life?

Client. Well, of course.

VBFP. Second, cold prospecting is expensive. Just like you, I have a financial strategy that requires money to fulfill. The time, energy, and money I invest in advertising or cold prospecting will have to be replaced somehow in order for my family to achieve our financial goals. It's a fact of life. Referrals are the least expensive and least time-consuming method for me to build my business, and I need your help.

If even one client chooses not to provide referrals, that puts a burden on the others to provide more referrals, or it means I have to institute those expensive advertising and prospecting campaigns. I am asking for your help because it is in both of our best interests.

I promise to handle your introductions in the same professional manner I have used with you. As few as five or ten introductions to start can help a lot.

Client.   I see your point. I'll do the best I can.

VBFP.   Great! Let's start with the client profile.

If the client is surprised by your asking for referrals at this point, the result may be resistance. The following dialogue helps you counter that type of resistance.

Client.   Why didn't you tell me up front about referrals?

VBFP. Two reasons. Number one: Talking about referrals with prospective clients is premature. When we first met, I wasn't sure we would have a basis for working together; therefore, I *couldn't* know whether I would want introductions to your friends and colleagues. Providing referrals was never a condition of our relationship. It's just smart.

Number two: Frankly, it never occurred to me that someone who is happy enough with my services to become a client would be reluctant to introduce me to their friends or colleagues. If you didn't value my services, you wouldn't have become a client in the first place. Are you uncomfortable with any aspect of how we have done business?

Client. No.

VBFP. Do you feel good about the work we have done?

Client. Yes.

VBFP. Then please help me help other people like you who need these services. And, for both our benefit, don't force me to use precious time on cold marketing strategies. It makes much more sense for me to invest my time staying on top of smart money strategies for you.

Let's begin with my target client
profile.

Client. OK.

Remember: If a new client has agreed to
implement your recommendations but refuses
to provide referrals, either you have failed to
create sufficient trust or your client is simply
not very impressed with the work that you have
done. Expect continuing problems in the client
relationship until you have established this
level of trust or you have impressed your client
with your competence.

This referral approach is not a gimmick. It is
a part of your intelligent business development
strategy, and it is a reflection of your capacity to
be totally honest with your client.

Still Afraid to Ask for Referrals?

Consider the story of Typical Tom. He has
300 clients who were garnered from his few
years of random prospecting and marketing.
Only 30 of them are really Great Clients. He
would like to have more clients just like them,
so he has experimented with cold-calls, done
a little direct mail, conducted a handful of
seminars, attended some networking functions
and occasionally gets referrals. His business
fluctuates from month to month, and when he
is seeing lots of people his prospect pipeline dries
up. Once that happens he cranks up another
prospecting "campaign." It's the typical cycle.

Tom averages about 10 new clients every 90
days whose profiles are a lot like his existing
300: 1 who is really great and 9 who buy just a
product or two. After 90 days he has only 31

clients who represent his true target, and he has to start over again with yet another prospecting campaign. These campaigns are sometimes expensive, always time consuming, take a lot of energy and yield about the same results.

Industrious Ivan, on the other hand, has decided there has to be a better way. He also has about 300 clients, but decides to focus only on the 30 Great Clients and try to get referrals from them. His biggest fear is that he will offend some of them by asking for referrals and they will take their business elsewhere. He hasn't actually heard of that ever happening, but he's afraid nonetheless. Fortunately, he's so frustrated with his current methods that he will try this new referral strategy no matter what. He calls his 30 best clients and sets appointments with them.

Typical Tom spends lots of time cold-calling and running prospecting "campaigns."

Ivan meets with all 30 Great Clients. He tells them the truth about his business, shows them his Ideal Client Profile and asks for their help. His worst fear comes true with five of them! Five of his best clients actually tell him to take a hike. They not only refuse to provide referrals, but they transfer their accounts to a competitor. The other 25, however, are impressed with his professional approach and were happy to introduce Ivan to an average of five people each who meet his ideal client profile. Ivan would normally have been very upset about losing five of his best clients, but he is too busy preparing the value-added campaign for his

125 hot, referred prospects and getting ready to call them.

Over the course of the next two months Ivan makes contact with all 125. Even though this is new to Ivan and he isn't super-skilled at converting hot, referred prospects into appointments, Ivan manages to get half of them (62) to agree to meet with him. Ivan is still perfecting his values-based interview skills, so of the 62 who meet with him only half (31) become clients. That's 31 new clients in 90–120 days who all meet his ideal client profile—and all referred from his best clients. Ivan is amazed at how simple it was to almost double the number of Great Clients in just a few months (30 minus the 5 who left = 25, plus the 31 new clients = 56).

He wishes only that he had become frustrated much sooner. He thinks about the five clients he lost with amusement because he knows Typical Tom would probably consider shooting five of his best clients to get 31 who are as good or better.

Ivan's production no longer swings up and down with the ebb and flow of random prospecting and marketing because the 31 new clients each introduced him to five more people who meet his ideal client profile. In fact, it was very easy to get referrals from these clients because they had all come to him from a referral.

He has 155 (31 × 5) hot, referred prospects in his system to contact and he's getting better and better at converting them into appointments. He's also getting quite good at the values-based interview so he anticipates much higher than the 50% conversion he experienced last time.

Pretty soon he will have to get rid of the bottom 90% of his clientele because it won't be fair to his best clients to keep them. But right now he thinks he'll enjoy the time off with his family and order another Mai Tai. After all, that's what he promised himself he would do when he became this successful.

ANOTHER MAI TAI PLEASE....

Look at Ivan now!

It takes 90–180 days to convert your business from expensive prospecting and marketing systems to the permanent momentum of a 100% referral-based business. Imagine what your life will be like when your clientele consists only of people who meet your ideal profile and come to you from referrals. Think of all the fees you will be earning, all the assets you will have under management, all the commissions and all the referrals you will continue to get. This is financial services nirvana . . . and it's possible for you. Earn your clients' trust, impress them with the quality of your work, coach them to implement strategies that will achieve their goals and fulfill their values, maintain trust, add value and ask for referrals.

E. How to Handle Resistance on the Phone

If you call a referred prospect and get an immediate negative reaction, the negativity isn't about you personally—the prospect doesn't know you personally. At this point, you may be facing just a normal reaction: He or she is qualifying you to decide whether or not to meet with you. Then again, the prospect may be adamantly resisting and not worth the trouble of meeting. You need to decide at some point, if the prospect does not seem receptive, whether that person can be moved to receptivity. Consider the following dialogue between a Values-Based Financial Professional (VBFP) and a prospect, which will lead to an emotional shift if the prospect can be moved to receptivity.

Prospect. Well, gee, we really don't want to get together with you.

VBFP. I understand. You get a lot of calls like this. Maybe you really do want to meet with me and don't know how to decide whether I'm just one of the many people who call you or whether I'm someone worth meeting. You sound like a reasonably bright person who would like to meet with me if you knew for sure that I would help you and add value to your life. But right now you have no idea whether I'm one of the many people who are really pretty useless to you or whether I'm one of the small minority who does have something to offer you.

I'm smart enough to understand this problem, and you're bright enough to figure out if you want to meet with me, so why don't we spend five minutes on the phone and determine whether I can add value to your life?

Often, the prospect is so surprised and interested by this type of unusual response that you can move easily into the values conversation. Moreover, setting an appointment is almost assured even before the values conversation takes place.

Three Common Questions and Effective Answers

Sometimes, prospects feel they need clarification before they enter into the values conversation or before they set an appointment to meet with you. Three of the common questions asked are, "What do you do?" "Can you send me something?" and "What are you trying to sell?"

The dialogues below suggest ways to handle these questions.

"WHAT DO YOU DO?"

Prospect. What do you do?

VBFP.   Well, do you have a written financial strategy?

Prospect. Not exactly.

VBFP. I help people who are serious about achieving their financial goals align the most intelligent financial choices with their goals.

Prospect. How do you do that?

VBFP. That depends. If you want to invest just another few minutes on the phone, we can probably at least determine how we would do that for you and if there is any benefit to us getting together. Would you like to do that now?

Prospect. Sure, why not?

VBFP. The first step of the process is for me to clearly understand the importance of money to each individual I work with. Give me your perspective. What's important about money *to you*?

[*Proceeding with the values conversation as described in Chapter 2, then redirecting the conversation when it is confirmed that the prospect has named the highest value and restating prospect's values in their own words.*]

Suppose we were able to create a very specific written strategy that helps you make the smartest financial choices so you can ———.
Are you interested in discovering how that would work?

Prospect. Yes.

VBFP. From my perspective, you sound like the type of person whom I can help make smart financial choices and who can benefit from a working relationship with me. There is no charge for an initial consultation. I have some time available in my calendar next week. Which day is best for you and your spouse?

Notice the language of the VBFP, who tends to talk in terms of *process, plan, strategy, idea, methods* and *systems*. All the language supports the direction that the VBFP wants to go. If you change process to product or you change strategy to service, you lose that direction. Using the most effective words is crucial.

"CAN YOU SEND ME SOMETHING?"

Prospect. Can you send me something?

VBFP. There really isn't anything to send. Creating a financial strategy is a very personal thing. To truly understand how it works it's important to *experience* it for yourself. It sounds like there might be some things I can do to help you make smart financial choices. I give advice for a living. The first piece of advice I have to offer is for you to take me up on my no-cost offer and discover for yourself

how this works. I have some time
in my calendar next week.
Is there a day that works best
for you?

OR

VBFP.   Are you asking me to send you
something in the mail because
you are sincerely interested in
finding out how my process
might help you make smart financial choices, or are you just trying
to politely get rid of me?

Prospect. I'm sincerely trying to figure out
if we should meet or not.

VBFP.   I can send you a free copy of our
book on financial strategizing.
Would you like me to do that?

If the answer is that he or she is trying to
get rid of you politely, allow it to happen.
Proceed to the next referred prospect.

OR

VBFP.   Because financial planning
involves so many individual decisions, there's really no general
information that we send out to
everybody. However, we do present free seminars on financial
strategizing; perhaps you would
prefer to attend a seminar to find
out who we are and what we do.
Would you like to sign up for one
of our seminars?

OR

VBFP. I would be happy to send something in the mail. I have made an audiotape* overview of how I work with my clients. I can send that tape to you at no charge. First, can I ask you a very direct question?

Prospect. Sure.

VBFP. Are you asking me to send you something in the mail because you are sincerely interested in finding out how my process might help you make smart financial choices, or are you just trying to politely get rid of me?

Prospect. I'm sincerely trying to figure out if we should meet or not.

If the answer is that he or she is trying to get rid of you politely, allow it to happen. Proceed to the next referred prospect.

VBFP. Great. Do you have a cassette player in your car?

Prospect. Yes.

VBFP. If I promise to send you this audiotape, will you promise to listen to it and give me your honest feedback about the service and process described on the tape?

If you are interested in creating an Audio Business Card, contact Cold Call Cowboy Productions, (760) 568-5124. Or for an Audio Brochure, call (800) 817-8912.

Prospect. Yes.

VBFP.   Is one week enough time for you to listen to the tape?

Prospect. Yes.

VBFP.   It will take a day or two for the tape to get to you. Do you have your calendar or schedule handy?

Prospect. Yes.

VBFP.   How about if we schedule a phone appointment for nine days from now, on [*date*]? What time works best for you?

Prospect. Can't you just call me sometime that day?

VBFP.   No, I really can't do that. My schedule is quite busy, and I'm sure yours is, too. So neither of us can afford to play "telephone tag." You know what that's like; sometimes you spend more time calling back and forth than the whole conversation will take. Let's just set a specific time, and we won't have to worry about that problem. What time is good for you?

"WHAT ARE YOU TRYING TO SELL?"

Prospect. What are you trying to sell?

VBFP. People buy various financial services from me, but I really don't sell anything. At this point, I don't know enough about you to know how or if I can help you, and you don't know enough about me to know that I can't. I suggest we meet or have a short discussion right now to figure that out.

All Paths Lead to the Values Conversation.

On the phone or in the office, when prospects use irrelevant questions to sidestep the values conversation, I acknowledge and respond briefly to the question, then I bring them back on track to where I was going anyway. When any question occurs, the answer to that question leads into the values conversation. I've provided a few examples below.

Prospect. What's your current thinking about the deficit?

VBFP. Well, my current position on the deficit is that it is too high, but I try not to spend too much time worrying about issues over which I have no control. What I want to do is help my clients make smart choices. In order to do that, I must understand each one's perspective on money. What's important about money *to you?*

Prospect. What do you think about Greenspan and how he's handling interest rates?

VBFP. Well, I think sometimes he handles them right and some-times he doesn't. What's really important is that I know how my clients handle their money. In order to do that, I have to understand what's important about money to each of them. What's your perspective? What's important about money *to you?*

Prospect. So, how long have you been in this business?

VBFP. I've been in the business about —— years. During that time, I've helped a lot of people make smart financial choices about their money. Help me understand your perspective. What's important about money *to you?*

Prospect. Hey, what stocks do you own right now?

VBFP. I have a variety of stocks. But the question is not really which stocks I own but which stocks are right for you. In order for me to determine that, I need to understand this first: What's important about money *to you?*

Prospect. How can I possibly save money when I must pay all these taxes?

VBFP. To answer that, the first step is to find some reason that will help you perceive your money in a way that's constructive. What's important about money *to you?*

If you were totally focused on getting to a certain city, you'd find a way to get there. If you are totally focused on conducting the values conversation, you will adroitly, briefly answer the irrelevant questions and lead the prospect back to the path of the values conversation.

About the Author

ill Bachrach, CSP is one of the foremost success resources for the financial services industry. Bill's personal success in our business is apparent in everything he teaches. Bill's best-selling book *Values-Based Selling; The Art of Building High-Trust Client Relationships* is considered a "must read" book in our business. He created the Values-Based Selling™ Mastery System, The Values-Based Selling™ Academy, the Trusted Advisor Coach® program, and the Being Done™ Study Group. He co-authored *High-Trust Leadership* with Norman Levine to help leaders implement a values-based approach for recruiting and managing Trusted Advisors™. His latest book *Values-Based Financial Planning* teaches consumers how to align their financial choices with their personal core values and how to make the best decision about doing it themselves or hiring a Trusted Advisor™.

Bill is considered to be the industry's leading resource for helping financial professionals make the transition from being salespeople to being Trusted Advisors™. In January of 2001 the readers of *Financial Planning Magazine* named Bill Bachrach as one of the four most influential people in our business.

It would be hard to find a financial services firm who has not hired Bill Bachrach to make a presentation or a respected financial services magazine that has not published one or more of his articles. He has given well over 1000 presentations worldwide, including seven presentations at the Financial Planning Association's National Convention, four appearances at the Million Dollar Round Table Annual meeting, and Top of the Table.

On a personal note, in 1998 Bill successfully completed the Hawaii Ironman Triathlon. The 2.4 mile swim, 112 mile bike, and 26.2 mile marathon run held annually in hot, windy, rugged volcanic terrain is considered to be the toughest single-day athletic event in the world.

Bill lives in San Diego with his wife, Anne, who helped him build his business.

About Bachrach & Associates, Inc.

The Strategic Objective of Bachrach & Associates, Inc. is to transform financial professionals from successful salespeople to mega-successful Trusted Advisors™.

After 15 years of development, implementation, and refinement the results speak for themselves. Financial Professionals who implement Bachrach's Values-Based Selling™ & Values-Based Financial Planning™ methods create first interview *experiences* so profound that 5 things *naturally* occur:

1. People hire you to create a written financial plan and pay whatever you ask.

2. They give you all their money and stop working with other advisors.

3. They ignore "financial pornography."

4. They do whatever you tell them to do.

5. They introduce you to everyone they know who meets your Ideal Client Profile.

This is not the promise of benefits from cleverly written marketing material. These are the proven facts of what happens for advisors who abandon traditional sales techniques and learn to behave like a Trusted Advisor™.

Bachrach & Associates, Inc. has the tools to help individual financial professionals make the transition to being Trusted Advisors™. We also have resources to help financial institutions integrate Values-Based Selling™ into their cultures to bring an entire organization of Trusted Advisors™ to their clients.

8380 Miramar Mall, Suite 200
San Diego, CA 92121
Tel. (800) 347-3707
Fax (858) 558-0748
E-mail: info@BachrachVBS.com
http://www.BachrachVBS.com

Additional Resources from Bachrach & Associates, Inc.

For a fraction of the value of one good client,
you will enjoy a lifetime of results from the

Values-Based Selling™ Mastery System!

You Get It All! *for only $599*

- *Values-Based Selling* book
- *Values-Based Selling*™ audios
- Values Conversation™ and Financial Road Map® Video Tapes
- Coaching & Follow-up: 4 Group Quarterly Teleconferences with Bill Bachrach

- Financial Road Maps® (package of 25)
- Financial Road Map® (laminated poster for use with dry erasable markers)
- *Values-Based Financial Planning* book

Don't wait . . . Order Today!

Values Conversation™ and Financial Road Map® Training Videos

If a picture is worth a thousand words, these video tapes can be worth hundreds of thousands of dollars. There's nothing more powerful than watching the master in action.

On these 3 1/2 hours of videotape, Bill demonstrates every situation you will encounter on your way to taking great client relationships to the highest possible level so that they:

- *Hire you to write a plan*

- *Give you all their money*

- *Ignore Financial Pornography*

- *Do what you tell them to do*

- *Give you referrals*

Only $159 each!

Bill will show you how to turn apparently difficult situations into golden opportunities.

You will also see two demonstrations of the entire Financial Road Map® interview with a pre-retirement "baby-boomer" couple and a wealthy retired couple, from the opening of the meeting to getting the check.

These videos will dramatically accelerate your understanding and mastery of the Values Conversation™ and the Financial Road Map®.

Mail us the reply card in the back of this book or call (800) 347-3707 to purchase.

Financial Road Map®
A Vital Tool for Inspiring Your Clients to Action

The value of a compelling visual representation of clients' values, goals and current financial reality cannot be underestimated. Bachrach & Associates, Inc. now offers the Financial Road Map® featured in this book in a big (27" x 39") laminated poster for use with erasable markers. It's ideal for client meetings and presentations. PRICE $99.

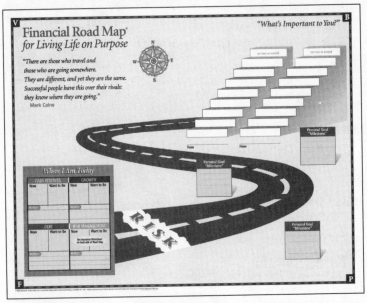

The Financial Road Map® is also available in a 17" x 22" version for desktop use—clients can keep the original and you can keep a copy in your file. The back can be used as a simple fact-finder. PRICE $29 FOR PACKAGE OF 25 MAPS.

Call (800) 347-3707 now for a free sample, or mail us the reply card in the back of this book to purchase.

The Winning Spirit
A Book of Championship Caliber

"If your profession were an Olympic event, would you make the team?" Bill Bachrach asks in the first chapter of this extraordinary book of short essays by 20 of the country's finest motivational speakers. Inspired by the determination, spirit and will of Olympic athletes, *The Winning Spirit* considers these same qualities in terms of daily life. In addition to Bill Bachrach's essay, "Olympic Thinking," contributions include

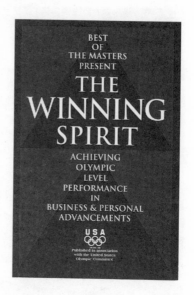

- Jim Tunney on "Mental Biceps,"
- Tony Alessandra on "Take Aim in Life,"
- George Walther on "Win the Gold With Mettle,"
- Bill Brooks on "How to Be Your Own Olympic Coach,"
- Jim Cathcart on "Helping People Grow,"
- Les Brown on "Olympic Dreams."

The Winning Spirit was published in association with the United States Olympic Committee. PRICE $16.95

Mail us the reply card in the back of this book or call (800) 347-3707 to purchase.

Success Road Map®

A Vital Tool for Inspiring Existing Producers to Action and for Recruiting

The value of a compelling visual representation of values, goals and current business reality cannot be underestimated.

The **Success Road Map**® is available in a 17" x 22" version for desktop use—producers can keep the original and the leader can keep a copy in the file. The back includes the 9 Core Competencies and planning worksheet, as taught in *High-Trust Leadership*.

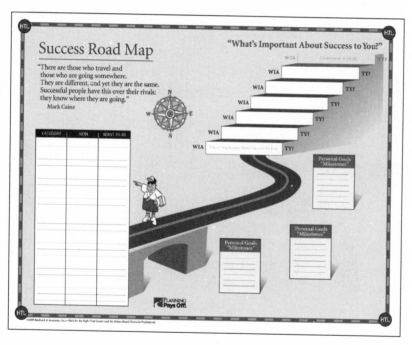

PRICE $29 FOR PACKAGE OF 25 MAPS.

Call (800) 347-3707 now for a free sample, or mail us the reply form in the back of this section to purchase.

Instead of wishing things would get easier,
start looking at how you can get better.

Don't be a salesperson.
Be a Trusted Advisor™.
Get More Clients! Get Better Clients!

Get skilled at our proven 5-conversation process that will **inspire your prospects and existing clients to:**

1. Hire you to write a plan
2. Give you all of their money
3. Ignore Financial Pornography
4. Follow your advice
5. Give you more referrals

MORE SKILL = MORE RESULTS.

At the **Values-Based Selling™ Academy,** you will increase your skill with the Financial Road Map® interview. You will **rehearse it, practice it, and get feedback.** You will get answers to your questions and deal with challenges on the spot. By the end of this 3-day, highly interactive, learning experience you will have honed your client interview skills to a new level and have the confidence to consistently **behave like a Trusted Advisor™ every day** for the rest of your career. It's down to earth and **you get big results.** You will invest more time working on your client interview than most financial professionals spend in a lifetime. Your **competitive advantage, skill and confidence** will allow you to prosper at a level of success that most financial professionals only fantasize about. No matter how successful you are today Bill Bachrach has the skill, the knowledge, and the experience to help you **go to the next level.**

360

Why Invest Three Days Perfecting Your Client Interview?

The client interview is as much the core skill for financial professionals as the golf swing is for the pro golfer. The client interview is where you build trust, get complete financial disclosure, and get the commitments that **make you money and deliver value to your clients.** It is also where you build the relationships that create a steady flow of referrals so you can **spend less time prospecting and marketing, and more time helping clients.** Of course, the most important aspect of the interview is the quality of the questions and your ability to truly listen. We think listening well is the key to earning peoples' trust.

Practical content you can use immediately to produce results.
Delivered in a fun, energetic, and inspiring style.

"At a time when so many of my colleagues are producing less, my income is up 18.6% A big part of this result is due to what I learned from Bill Bachrach. I only need 11 more clients and I'm done."

–BRIAN FRICKE • RIA

You will learn to use the simple, compelling, visual tool called the Financial Road Map® that has helped other advisors like you become million-dollar producers on an accelerated time schedule.

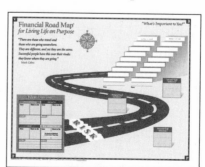

Bill will teach you . . .

- How to prospect for new clients in a way that positions you as a Trusted Advisor™, not a product salesperson.

- Specific strategies for getting the best clients when the markets are down and their investments have declined in value. (We've heard there's a recession and we encourage you to choose not to participate!)

- How to build your business with "A" clients only.

- How to transition your clients from the "old world" of paying commissions to the "new world" of paying you annual recurring revenue.

- The magic of "Being Done." You will learn how to structure your business to earn all the money you will ever need or want from a finite number of clients who pay you a predictable amount of revenue to be their Trusted Advisor™.

- How to get off the prospecting and marketing treadmill and get quality ideal clients faster.

BILL BACHRACH is the creator of The Values-Based Selling™ Mastery System, The Values-Based Selling™ Academy, The Trusted Advisor Coach® program, and Values-Based Financial Planning™. His programs are considered to be the most effective in the industry for helping financial professionals transition from being salespeople to Trusted Advisors™. His best-selling book, *Values-Based Selling: The Art of Building High-Trust Client Relationships for Financial Professionals,* is one of the must-read books in our business. He has conducted over 1000 seminars, workshops, and keynote speeches, including multiple appearances at the Financial Planning Association, the Million Dollar Round Table, Top of the Table and hundreds of corporate and association events worldwide.

"My colleagues were shocked when I told them that I don't have any Bs and Cs. Thanks to my work with Bill Bachrach I only have A clients."

— GARY MOORE
Merrill Lynch

The ultimate objective is to BE DONE.

Being Done™ means that you have a finite number of loyal clients who happily pay you recurring revenue every year, so you virtually never have to prospect and market again.

Lots of content and lots of practice.

DAY ONE	DAY TWO	DAY THREE
• Trust training vs. sales training. • The evolution of where we have been, where we are, and how to be a Trusted Advisor™. • The Trusted Advisor™ payoff: more business, more personal income, more referrals, more assets and better quality of life. • Lots of Values Conversation™ practice, practice, practice. • How to deal with the ten most common issues and obstacles to mastering the Values Conversation™.	• The four key components of a successful goals conversation. • Handling financial documents with skill, finesse, and competence. • Organizing their financial information in a simple, inspiring way. • How to get commitment to hire you in the first meeting. • How to get their commitment to implement before you go to work, so they take action at the next meeting. You will never go to work and not get paid for it again.	• Practice the entire client interview. • Q&A with Bill Bachrach. • The simplest referral dialogue on the planet that works only for Trusted Advisors™. • Learn a simple phone dialogue and process that will fill your appointment calendar with the right prospects. • Action plan: Bill will guide you through your personal action plan so you take what you have learned in this workshop to produce results fast.
By the end of day one you will be skilled and confident with the Values Conversation™ so people are inspired to hire you based on their own clarity of values.	*By the end of day two you will be skilled in and confident to conduct all five conversations of the Financial Road Map® interview.*	*By the end of day three, you will put it all together and have an action plan to implement what you've learned to get more ideal clients.*

The Trusted Advisor Coach®—
for Successful Financial Professionals Who Seek Perfection in the Client Interview

With the same principles professional athletes use to make small adjustments that produce large performance gains, Bill Bachrach has created a one-year coaching process using video tape, intense coaching and feedback.

This program is proven to help very successful financial professionals produce more results in far less time. You will finally discover *exactly* why clients do business with you because, if you are honest with yourself, you probably don't really know.
Isn't it time you did?

To qualify, you must

- show proof of a personal annual income in excess of $100,000,

- be open to frank evaluation of your skills,

- be very good at the client interview right now,

- be familiar with Values-Based Selling™,

- have big goals and a secure ego.

Big goals means income in excess of $250,000, $500,000, $1,000,000 or more. It means two to four months per year of free time. It means a quality of life that includes total goal achievement and values fulfillment. It means truly making a difference in the lives of others. *continued next page*

> *"The Trusted Advisor Coach® program has helped me to get laser focused on my ideal clients and develop the skills necessary to get them as clients. In one month alone I have gotten three accounts worth over one million dollars."*
>
> **Keith Cline,** Raymond James & Associates, Inc.

- [ ] Do you still discover assets months or years into the relationship?
- [ ] Do you still fall back on old-fashioned rapport-building techniques?
- [ ] Do your interviews take longer than one hour?
- [ ] Do you have to meet with people more than once before they make a commitment to do business with you?
- [ ] Do you have time in your calendar to see more people?
- [ ] Do you have several hundred clients, yet still use conventional prospecting and marketing techniques (e.g., telemarketing, newspaper ads, networking)?
- [ ] Do you call the office on your days off or bring work with you on vacation?
- [ ] Do you take less than three months of vacation every year?

"Using what I learned at the first TAC session I was able to generate revenues which are twice as much as the whole of last year in just six months."

Mayur Dalal
Legacy Planning Group, LLC

If you answered yes to any of these questions, you may be good, but your interview skills are not perfect yet.

Because there are few resources and little support in the financial services industry for people who choose to operate at your level, The Trusted Advisor Coach® is an exclusive skill development process designed specifically for you. There are no gimmicks or cute techniques. Just smart work, intense coaching, lots of feedback and real-world application. Using the strategies of elite athletes and interaction with your peers, you will move to a level most financial professionals can't even imagine.

Mail us the reply card in the back of this book or call (800) 347-3707 for further information or to apply today.

Values-Based Financial Planning
*The Next Step in Revolutionizing
Your Business—
And the Financial Services Industry*

For the first time ever, the general public has a book to help them understand the unique value of creating a values-based Financial Road Map® and discover how important it is to have a trusted advisor who is a Values-Based Financial Professional™. With *Values-Based Financial Planning*, financial services consumers can

- realize what's most important to them and align their financial choices with their core values so they can have the great lives they want,

- become inspired to do whatever it takes to live the lives they dream of,

- decide if they're ready to stop worrying about their money and start delegating its management to a competent professional (you!),

- follow the step-by-step process to build their own Financial Road Map®—or discover how important it is to have a Values-Based Financial Professional™ help them build it,

- understand how top financial advisors view clients so they can be the kind of person who gets the best service,

- and much more!

As a Trusted Advisor™, you already know that the keys to building your business are the referrals you receive from your most respected clients—and your ability to determine which of those referred people are equipped to appreciate your services and implement the plan you create for them. Now you can provide them the best possible information about how you do business, helping them discover if there's a natural fit with your practice, or not. *Values-Based Financial Planning* delivers straight into their hands the exact expectations, processes, and principles that are integral to your successful business. You can

- purchase quantities of *Values-Based Financial Planning* at a volume discount,

- write a customized introduction to be bound into the front of the books (with a minimum order of 500 copies),

- and give each core client at least five copies to deliver to family and friends who meet your Ideal Client Profile.

The perfect marketing complement to providing your clients with the *Values-Based Financial Planning* book, its companion newsletter brings valuable ideas and information right to their

doors every month. With this monthly publication that we customize with your business information and you mail to your clients, you stay in touch every 30 days. The purpose of the newsletter is not, however, to market specific services or products offered by you or your firm; it is to provide articles of interest to anyone who is committed to having a high quality of life.

Trusted Advisors™ who've implemented this turnkey system – sending clients both the *Values-Based Financial Planning* book and newsletter – tell us they experience both the gratification of a genuine, "value-added" marketing strategy, as well as impressive results with referrals.

Please call (800) 347-3707 for pricing information.

To order your custom copies, or to inquire about our
Values-Based Financial Planning™ *seminar licensing*
program, call 800-347-3707.

Bibliography

Applebaum, Judith and Nancy Evans. *How to Get Happily Published.* New York: HarperCollins, 1992.

Blanchard, Ken and Don Shula. *Everyone's a Coach: You Can Inspire Anyone to Be a Winner.* Grand Rapids, MI: Zondervan Publishing House, 1995.

Burgett, Gordon. *Niche Marketing for Writers, Speakers, and Entrepreneurs.* Santa Maria: Communication Unlimited, 1993.

——————. *Self-Publishing to Tightly Targeted Markets.* Santa Maria: Communication Unlimited, 1989.

Covey, Stephen R. *The 7 Habits of Highly Effective People.* New York: Simon & Schuster, 1989.

Giles, Sarah. *Fred Astaire—His Friends Talk.* New York: Doubleday, 1988.

Griffith, Joe. *Speaker's Library of Business Stories, Anecdotes, and Humor.* Englewood Cliffs: Prentice Hall, Inc., 1990.

Kuralt, Charles. *Charles Kuralt's America.* New York: G. P. Putnam's Sons, 1995.

Leonard, George. *Mastery.* New York: Penguin Books USA, Inc., 1992.

Mackay, Harvey. *Swim With the Sharks Without Being Eaten Alive.* New York: William Morrow and Company, Inc., 1988.

Poynter, Dan. *The Self-Publishing Manual: How to Write, Print and Sell Your Own Book*, 8th revised edition. Santa Barbara: Para Publishing, 1995.

Ross, Marilyn and Tom Ross. *The Complete Guide to Self-Publishing.* Cincinnati: Writer's Digest Books, 1994.

Treacy, Michael and Fred Wiersema. *The Discipline of the Market Leaders.* Reading, MA: Addison-Wesley Publishing Company, 1995.

Willette, Anne. "You'll Need $1 Million to Retire." *USA Today,* May 8, 1985, page 1A.

Zinsser, William. *On Writing Well*, 5th edition. New York: HarperCollins, 1994.

INDEX

M

N

O

P

Q

R

S

BACHRACH & ASSOCIATES, INC. PRODUCT ORDER FORM

ITEM (Volume discounts available on all items—call for details)	QTY	UNIT PRICE	TOTAL
The Mastery System Get it all, and save over $409!		~~$1,008.90~~ **$599.**⁰⁰	
Values Conversation™ Training Video 90 minutes of Values Conversation demonstrations		$159.00	
Financial Road Map® Training Video 2 hours of Financial Road Map demonstrations		$159.00	
Values-Based Selling™ Audio Cassette Series 8+ hours on 8 audio tapes		$199.00	
Values-Based Selling book		$34.95	
Financial Road Map® (22" x 17") Package of 25, paper, for desktop use		$29.00	
Financial Road Map® (39" x 27") Laminated poster; use with dry erase markers		$99.00	
The Values-Based Financial Planning book Customization available: call for details		$29.95	
Teleconference Renewal 4 quarterly calls Available to Mastery System owners only		$299.00	
High-Trust Leadership book		$27.95	
Success Road Map® (22" x 17") Package of 25, paper, for desktop use		$29.00	
The Winning Spirit book Opening chapter by Bill Bachrach, published in association with the U.S. Olympic Committee		$16.95	
Quality of Life Enhancer Worksheets (pad 50)		$19.95	
The Values-Based Financial Planning™ Newsletter		(Call for price)	
	SUBTOTAL		
	7.75% SALES TAX (California residents only)		
	SHIPPING (See chart)		
	TOTAL All funds U.S. dollars	**$**	

To order call
(800) 347-3707,
visit our website at
www.bachrachvbs.com,
or photocopy
this form and mail to:

Bachrach & Associates, Inc.
8380 Miramar Mall,
Suite 200
San Diego, CA 92121

— or fax to —

(858) 558-0748.

Thank You!

U.S. SHIPPING & HANDLING

(call for charges outside U.S. or to expedite shipping):

Orders are shipped UPS GROUND.

For orders
up to $50 .... $ 7.00
$51–$100 .... $15.00
$101–$300 .... $20.00
$301–$600 .... $35.00
Over $600
call for price

If you desire express delivery, please call us for assistance. International shipping additional. Does not include customs or brokerage fees.

Rev. 2/2002 • This order form supercedes all previous forms. Prices subject to change.

BACHRACH
ASSOCIATES • INC
Values-Based Selling™

❑ **Here's my check** (payable to Bachrach & Associates, Inc.).

Please charge my: ❑ American Express ❑ Visa ❑ MasterCard ❑ Discover

Card # _____ Expires _____

Signature _____

Name _____

Company _____

Address _____

City _____ State _____ Zip _____

Phone (____) _____ Fax (____) _____

e-mail _____

'd like to know more! Please call me about
❑ customized keynote speeches or workshops
❑ on-site training and consulting services
❑ customized *Values-Based Financial Planning* books

❑ add me to the content-rich free e-mail
❑ The Values-Based Selling™ Academy
❑ The Trusted Advisor Coach® program for top producers

NO POSTAGE
NECESSARY
IF MAILED
IN THE
UNITED STATES

Business Reply Mail

First Class Mail Permit No. 23595 San Diego, CA

Postage Will be Paid by Addressee

Bachrach & Associates, Inc.
8380 Miramar Mall, Suite 200
San Diego, CA 92121-2549